For Laurel —

May God's Peace
and Angel's Wings
Surround You!

Terry Lee Rombo

"Christmas 2010"

Troy's Miracles

by his mom

Terry Lee Rambo

C/P

CONTINENTAL SHELF PUBLISHING, LLC
Savannah, GA

Cover Art by Krystn Palmer
Photographs courtesy of author
Author Photograph: JC Penney Portrait Studios

Library of Congress Cataloging-in-Publication Data
Rambo, Terry Lee
 Troy's Miracles
  p. cm.

   Summary: "Grieving mother's memoir, who lost her son in a car accident. Coming to terms with her loss, she experiences odd coincidences culminating with messages from her son's spirit: small miracles to assure her that life goes on. From beyond the grave, spirit helps mother renew her faith and find peace at last."--Provided by publisher.

Softcover ISBN 978-0-9822583-8-5 (pbk. : alk. paper)
Hardcover ISBN 978-0-9822583-9-2 (pbk. : alk. paper)

Continental Shelf Publishing books are available at special quantity discounts for premiums, sales promotions, or use in educational, corporate and community training programs. For information, please contact: Sales@CSPBooks.com

For book signings, please contact Terry Lee Rambo at:
terrylee53@gmail.com

Printed in Canada
First Edition, December 2010

Dedicated To

My Special Mom - Shirley Fay
My Precious Daughter - Terra Fay
My Grandchildren: Jaidan, DanTerrah, Tobin & Karsynn
My Brothers and Sisters: Billy, Joe, Janice & Roxanne
All future generations

In Loving Memory Of

Thomas "Troy" Mills
Granddaddy and Mamareney Ruark
Great Grandmother Barrett

Contents

Introduction

    I was born Terry Lee Rhodes on October 5, 1953 in a little spot in northwestern Kentucky on the Ohio river called Uniontown, which would immediately mark me as a local "river rat." Me being the oldest of five children with two brothers coming close behind and two sisters bringing up the rear. We walked a few short blocks to the catholic school until graduating from 8th grade; however, since the catholic school had been closed down we had the adventure of finishing up our education with the public children. That was a whole new ball game.

    Fortunately, we had a multitude of family members living all around us, the greatest being our maternal grandparents and great grandmother just across the street. We had many wonderful years running back and forth between the two houses and out to the farm where granddaddy raised cattle, hogs, chickens, corn and wheat. There was always tons of love to keep us warm and summers filled with corn on the cob, tomatoes, watermelon, tag you're it and hide and seek. From the outside looking in we were a wonderful family, however, our father had a very dark side to him that would result in the cops toting him off to jail in handcuffs when I was 13 years old. My special mother, brothers and sisters all agree that it was the most wonderful day of our lives!

That next summer and many summers after that I would be fortunate enough to spend in California with my Aunt June and cousins Terri, Bobbi and Avery. After those somewhat adventurous summers I would never again be satisfied in the little "river rat town" that made me strong.

I felt way too mature for the kids I went to high school with and was in a big hurry to do and try everything the world had to offer. I quit in the 10th grade, went back then quit again in the 11th. The GED was much quicker and I could get on with living. For the first few years I bounced around from one thing to the next.

My first job was ironing button down men's shirts at the local dry cleaners for 10 cents each. After that I did one stint at the Dairy Mart then moved on up to the Dairy Maid where most of the kids hung out. It was fun but I needed more money so at 16 years of age, still attending high school, I went to work at the factory on midnight shift where I only worked a couple of weeks before someone recognized me and turned me into management for being too young. Sadly, I found out what it was like to be fired. Luckily the owner of the Dairy Maid offered me $1.25 per hour to come back. I realized I really was a good worker and cheerfully took her up on the offer. Eventually I got bored with it and tried to enlist in the United States Air Force but was told I was too young. Going back to the factory when I turned 18, I worked two weeks, decided that was not my cup of tea and turned in my resignation smiling to myself as I went out their door.

Like most young girls I dreamed of being a stewardess and enrolled in the Atlantic Airline School in Kansas City, Missouri. It was a blast staying in a huge old apartment building with roommates and even more so when we ventured across the state line into Kansas City, Kansas where you only had to be 18 to enter the bars and party. Unfortunately, I found out too late that I would have to attend another school if I wanted to continue my dreams of being a stewardess as this one only taught the things you needed to be a reservation or travel agent.

Luckily, after graduation I was offered three positions. Two were with travel agents and the third was a civilian clerical position with the United States Marine/Navy corp. in Arlington, Virginia where I worked for 8 months then decided to interview with a new Congressman on Capitol Hill in Washington. After botching that up I decided it was time to get out of the city. I had to ship my things by bus as there was too much to take on the plane. Some guy showed up in a van to take me with my boxes in tow to the bus station with a bra hanging off his rear view mirror. I remember praying for angels at that point! He turned out to be one of the friendliest fellows I've ever had the opportunity to be afraid of and after dropping off my belongings at the Greyhound Bus station he delivered me back to my apartment safe and sound. That was the day I discovered you can't judge a person by their cover. I made it back to Kentucky in one piece where I landed a position doing clerical work at the job corps. Talk about boring.

Before I'd left for the airline school I'd been dating a man named Terry who had visited me while I was at school and also in Arlington. When we met he was fresh out of Vietnam and wild as a buck which attracted me immediately. The fact that we both had the same name added to the attraction. He was the only person I knew that could do donuts around the Dairy Maid in his Chevy to impress me and not hit a single car parked on either side! I sure loved driving that four in the floor. We picked up the relationship where we left off and it wasn't long before I was pregnant and we were married. Unfortunately, I soon realized he wasn't ready to settle down yet and I wasn't mature enough to stick around until he was. Seemed I was either too mature or not mature enough for this thing called life!

When our son Troy was nine months old he and I hopped on a plane to Las Vegas where I had an aunt and uncle. Didn't work out there so we went to spend some time with my cousin Bobbi in California where I took a job at a Bob's Big Boy restaurant. The thrill of being a waitress quickly diminished the night I had a table of more than a dozen people to take care of. I interviewed for a modeling job and was offered a chance to go out to a party Hugh Heffner was throwing that week-end. My sweet cousin talked me out of that adventure and shortly after, Terry showed up and hauled Troy and I back to Kentucky. It still didn't work out.

I filed for a divorce and packed up my old black and yellow Chevy. Troy had his first birthday on the road as we followed my mom, her husband and my brothers and sisters down the highway to Wyoming. Yep, I had adventure in my bones.

Hanna, Wyoming turned out to be even more of a tiny spot than Uniontown, Kentucky! However, it sure provided me with a lot of opportunities. I had fun bartending for a few months about 30 miles down the Interstate in Rawlins. It was during the time the government thought the aliens were mutilating all the cattle so there was a lot of interesting chatter going around. I dated a much older man that talked me into moving to Salt Lake City, Utah. My brother Billy helped me move and I remember going to look at an apartment that a Mormon lady wouldn't let me have because she obviously didn't think he was my brother and I definitely was not a Mormon!

I took a job as a cocktail waitress, then a dance instructor at the Arthur Murray School of dance. Didn't take long for me to figure out ball room dancing was definitely not for me! Give me country, jazz and rock and roll. From there I found a position at The Executive Modeling Studio where I was "supposed" to model and sell over priced contracts to unsuspecting young girls. I was soon feeling guilty about taking advantage of them and considered quitting. That materialized the day the owner was out of the shop and I took a call asking for a girl to come by a local upscale hotel for a modeling job. I went over and was offered several hundred dollars to escort and possibly go to bed with a gentleman that was flying in from out of town that evening. Talk about being naïve! It scared the jeepers out of me. Needless to say I left the hotel and never went back to the modeling studio. Fortunately for me, Terry showed up about that time and hauled Troy and I back to Kentucky. Course, I still couldn't stay put.

Back to Wyoming we went, only Terry went along this time. Bless his heart. He was sure trying hard. However, he was one of those home town boys and he just couldn't stay away. Being in Vietnam had made him long for his home state of Kentucky so off he went and he's still there. Can't say I blame him for finally giving up.

Next thing you know I was working for a construction company contracted out at the local underground coal mine. Didn't take long for me to work myself up from a laborer to a backhoe operator and I ran the loader when the regular operator was off for one reason or another. I'd finally found something I loved doing. Wouldn't you know the job would end and I'd get laid off? Am still mad at myself as a couple months earlier the mining company had asked if I wanted to be the first female to go underground in the state of Wyoming and I turned them down. As it turned out I got to be number three.

Talk about an adventure. Crawling through tunnels like a mole. I spent most of the time rock dusting, which consists of holding a high pressured hose that is spraying pulverized limestone all over the walls, floor and ceiling so there won't be a coal dust ignition. Had to hang on tight or it would knock me off my feet. Must say I had to laugh when it happened to the kid that was working for me. Next they put me down at the face where they were actually extracting the coal. I saw a man accidentally get smacked in the head with a sledge hammer and a chunk of coal fall off a wall and just barely miss the operator on the loader that was 1/3 the size of the chunk. Was even brave (or dumb) enough to ride the coal belt out one time. Thinking back I believe that was the dumbest thing I've done in my life. I grabbed the wire, jumped on and my helmet went flying off! Lucky for me I was able to grab it before it got tangled up and I don't even want to think of what could have happened at that point. I had to lay flat on my belly to ride up the slope and in one spot I barely cleared the roof. Grabbed a wire and jumped off just as I cleared the tunnel. Nope, wouldn't do that again if I had the chance. However, it was an adventure!

Unfortunately, my boss made a pass at me one day. I turned him down, the shift ended and I barely made it into the front door of my apartment before I was projectile vomiting, followed by diarrhea and dry heaves. For three days I literally thought I was going to die. I was so sick I could barely make it from the bed to the bathroom, much less the doctor. I felt like I'd had something put in my thermos. I thought, "There has to be something better than this" and decided not to go back to the mine.

There was a man named Dan working underground that I was interested in. We eventually married and decided it would be a good idea if I went to work at the local surface coal mine. Another adventure!

I've always loved to drive but never thought I'd be behind the wheel of 80 ton end dumps and 100 ton belly dumps. Still, I did enjoy it; though I can't say that I cared much for third shift. My boss's name was Danny and shortly after I started he decided to teach me how to back up the belly dump by sending me in the wrong direction. There I was at the end of the road, a steep slope on one side, a hill on the other side, a dump truck of dirt in front of me and a pitch black sky. I've been a great backer up ever since.

Dan was taken in an automobile accident four months after we were married. I quit the coal mine, Danny and I married ten months later in May of 1978 and I became a stepmother to a six year old little boy. Since he lived in Arizona with his mother on the Navajo reservation he was only with us occasionally but I grew to love him dearly. He and Troy grew up knowing what it was like to have a brother.

The next year Danny got fired and we left Wyoming. We moved to Farmington, New Mexico and Tucson, Arizona in search of work but finally ended up in Henderson, Kentucky where our daughter Terra was born and the only work my husband could find was in a convenience store. Next we were off to his hometown of Crooksville, Ohio where he found mining work again. A better opportunity came in Jourdanton, Texas where we fell in love with authentic Mexican food and became foster parents to a six year old girl named Billie and a 3 month old little boy named Christopher. It was a wonderful time. We had yours, mine, ours and theirs as Danny's son Darryl was with us also. We were attending the boy's baseball games and the house was full of children and laughter. Both Billie and Christopher were adopted to loving families and not realizing how hard it would be to let them go we decided not to do it anymore.

Danny got laid off his job and we headed back to Kentucky where he found a position operating a dragline for Pyramid coal mine in Beaver Dam and I worked as a casual mail carrier for the United States Post Office in Owensboro. It was a temporary position relieving the regulars so they could go on vacation. After being charged at by a big red Doberman and passing a house with three pit bulls that were luckily sleeping in the 90 degree temperature I decided it was not worth $5 per hour and turned in my mail bag at the end of the day. I have tremendous admiration for our mail carriers. We were in Kentucky for a couple of years when the company offered him a position managing a gold mine they had just bought in Lewistown, Montana.

We fell in love with the "Big Sky Country" and it was an exciting time. The company had a Lear jet they flew back and forth from Kentucky so they let us hop a ride to go visit family. Terra even got to sit up front with the pilot. We were living the good life and the kids were snow skiing, playing sports and making all kinds of great friends. We finally felt like we were home. We traveled to Hawaii, Mexico and Belize in Central America.

Next thing you know the gold mine was sold and Danny was working for a company out of Texas selling grease and traveling out of state five days out of seven. With the kids in school and him gone most of the time I decided to join the local ambulance service. It would turn out to be the happiest years of my life. I'd finally found my niche. I absolutely loved being down in the ditch at car wrecks, ripping vehicles apart, helping people and the thrill of not knowing what the day would bring. The first wreck I went on was for a bunch of carnival workers that had smashed their truck and RV. The guy sitting on the ditch bank had no idea he had a massive chunk of wood sticking out of his cheek. From that day on I was hooked and never missed a class or opportunity to be totally involved. I remember the day we got to rappel off the tall ancient school building. Me, the girl who was absolutely terrified of heights! Just before I went off the edge I said, "A girl's got to do what a girl's got to do! " Everyone had a good laugh and I found out rappelling was another avenue of excitement I enjoyed. Always did love a good challenge and I found the adventure I craved on the ambulance service.

I even made my television debut while serving. Montana Power made a commercial and needed the fire dept., police personnel and the ambulance service on scene with them. My best friend Deb and I were picked. We stood around for hours in full gear hanging onto heavy bags loaded with equipment just so I could say, "they did the right thing" at the appropriate time. Although it was a fun experience, I quickly realized it wasn't something that interested me in the least.

Unfortunately, it was only a part time on call position as the town was too small for a full time service. After 4 years I took a full time position as a city police dispatcher and was not able to work on the ambulance as much. It turned out to be a mistake. The stress of trying to please 13 officers, the public, and one ill-tempered dispatcher took its toll and I was relieved when Danny was offered a job in Sullivan, Indiana managing a surface coal mine. The 1996 move turned out to be the biggest mistake of our marriage.

Fortunately, Troy had graduated from his Montana high school where he had been a high jump star in his senior year and cleared the bar at 6'6". Terra was not so lucky. She had to leave her friends and cheerleading behind and enter 10th grade in a place where she knew no one. It was heartbreaking to see the changes in her and I found myself wishing we'd never left Montana. Terra graduated from high school, then from a business college. She and her husband Jeff live in Minnesota with their three beautiful children. Troy gave me a beautiful granddaughter.

The new position in Indiana took its toll on my husband also. He went from someone who had treated me like a queen for over 18 years to someone I didn't know. Prayer became my only vise. In 2002 Troy passed in an automobile accident down in Kentucky and in 2008 Danny divorced me after 30 years of marriage for a much younger woman.

This book is about the miraculous things that have happened since Troy passed. He was a very loving and headstrong little boy. In fact at a doctors visit when he was two years old the physician told me I was going to have my hands full raising that one! He was certainly right about that, however, what he didn't tell me and didn't know is that I was raising an angel in disguise. His grin could melt your heart and melt them he did.

I remember at his high school graduation in 1992. His step-grandfather got such a kick out of all the young gals dropping by to congratulate him that he started taking a count! At his funeral in 2002 his father, Terry, couldn't help but grin at all the girls in the audience with tears running down their cheeks. Yes, my Troy boy was special indeed and I didn't realize just how special until he was gone. This is a wonderful true story that will renew your faith and prove that they never really leave us.

Kentucky Boy

The Accident

The miracles started happening even before the accident. On October 10, 2002 Troy and his girlfriend, Shayna, came up from Kentucky to visit me in Indiana and brought their daughter, Jaidan, who was two and a half months old. I was doing something in the kitchen and Troy was keeping me company. I can't remember what we were discussing but he said he was going to heaven. I said, "You are, well how do you know?" He said, "Jesus told me and my dad's going too." So naturally I asked him if I was going also and he shot me that famous grin of his. I said, "just don't go too soon, I'd miss you too much!" If I had only known how quickly it was going to be I would have hung onto that last hug a lot longer.

I was in the process of remodeling his old room at the house and had torn out the small closet on one side. I'd decided to put a walk in closet on the other side so the bed and dresser could be arranged in what I thought would be a more functional and pleasing design. However, since I'd never done anything like this before on my own I was a little skeptical about building a new closet. Troy assured me he could take care of it.

The day they were going to leave he was lying on the floor being lazy and I was getting a little antsy wondering if the closet was going to get done. All of a sudden he just jumped up and headed for the bedroom. Next thing

I knew the closet was framed out perfectly. I was totally dumbfounded as I'd never known him to do any carpentry work. I asked, "Where in the world did you learn to do that?" He said, "Jesus taught me!" There was that big grin again. Sure glad I took a picture since it turned out to be his last. That was my boy, he loved Jesus. I later wondered if they weren't having a discussion when I thought he was lying on that floor just being lazy.

They packed up to leave. He gave me a kiss on the cheek, a great big hug and as always, told me he loved me. Then they noticed Jaidan's pacifier was missing so he went back in the house to look for it, came out and gave me another big hug and kiss and told me he loved me once again. He flashed me his big grin as he buckled his seatbelt knowing I'd fuss at him if he didn't.

Like always, I walked down the sidewalk in front of the house so I could wave good-bye as they drove off. That was the very first time he didn't wave good-bye when he was leaving as he was turning around in the seat taking care of his daughter. Now I believe he didn't give a final wave because he never really left.

About 3:30 on the morning of October 26, 2002 I awoke with an incredible pain in my chest and woke my husband to tell him I felt like I was dying! The crushing pain lasted only a few moments before I leaned over the side of the bed, vomited, and then fell into a deep sleep. Danny obviously took on the job of cleaning up the mess I'd made.

I woke to the ringing phone and realized he'd already left for work. The next few moments were a blur. I remember Troy's father, Terry, telling me that Troy had been killed in an automobile accident and hearing myself scream, "No God, not my baby boy!" It was the worst day of my life.

Troy and Shayna had watched the movie "The City of Angels" the night before. In the movie Nicolas Cage played Seth. Seth's main responsibility is to appear to those who are close to death and guide them to the next life. Sarah

McLaughlin's song "Angel" was in it. The last lines are, "You are pulled from the wreckage of your silent reverie in the arms of the Angel: may you find some comfort here. You're in the arms of the Angel: may you find some comfort here."

After the movie they went out dancing in Shawneetown, Illinois which was just across the Ohio River from Uniontown. When they were ready to leave Troy asked Shayna if it would be okay with her if he rode back with his friend who was alone since Shayna already had a friend to ride back with her. She said okay, drove home and fell asleep.

The guys were in a small pick-up truck that left the right side of the highway at a high rate of speed, hit a telephone pole and flipped several times. Although Troy was wearing his seat belt he was pronounced dead at the scene along with the driver. When I received a copy of the accident report I noticed the time the call came in to 911 was 3:30 in the morning. Only then did I realize I had been granted the gift of knowing exactly what my son went through in his last moments because I was right there with him. Having been an EMT I know the pain I felt in my chest was the same pain he felt as he took his last breath. I take comfort in knowing how quick it was over.

My only other child, my daughter Terra had been sleeping downstairs in the living room when she heard me scream and came running in. She collapsed on the bed next to me. She and Troy had been very close and I worried that she might lose the child she was carrying from the trauma as she started crying and experiencing pain in her abdomen. I called her dad home before going to the hospital. After a few hours of monitoring she was allowed to return home. By that time we had called everyone that needed to be called and were thinking about the funeral.

Mom and her husband drove down from Minnesota to stay with us along with my sister Janice and her husband from Missouri. The rest of my family lived close enough to drive down to the funeral home.

Troy's Last Picture

The Funeral

We lived in Indiana and the accident happened in Kentucky where his father lives so it would be a lot of driving back and forth as I wanted to be in my own bed at night. Nothing prepared me for seeing my first born child in a casket. Parents are supposed to leave this world before their children, not the other way around.

They had his hair combed back and he always wore it forward. It didn't even look like him! I'd always told him to wear his seat belt but when I noticed a big tear they'd tried to repair behind his ear I found myself wishing he hadn't had it on that night as it had obviously torn his neck and failed to save his life. He was in a suit and I wished he was in one of his Dallas Cowboy jerseys as he loved them so and usually had one on along with one of their caps.

In fact they were scheduled to play the Indianapolis Colts in Indy on November 17 and Troy had asked me to purchase a set of four tickets so he and his friends could pay me for them and go to the game together. He never made it to that game so his friends left his seat open and cheered just as he would have wanted them to. His best friend up in Indiana, Gary, said they had felt he was right there with them. Maybe he was.

I had the funeral director comb his hair down but it still didn't look much like my Troy boy. I was thankful I had brought a large display of photos that I'd just recently arranged in a 24" x 36" picture frame showing him from birth to the present time. It's funny how things just happen to take care of themselves sometimes. Everyone seemed to enjoy looking at the pictures and seeing his beautiful smile. I still couldn't believe I was there.

I was numb; I guess a better phrase would be I was in shock. I just wondered around. His dad very seldom left the casket. I wondered later if I was supposed to stand up there and greet people as he did. I still don't know what the proper etiquette is for burying a child but I couldn't stand up there next to the dead person in that casket.

Poor Terra, she couldn't even go up and look at him the first day. Not until they were ready to close it up the next day did she venture up to tell him good-bye and collect the gold cross he always wore around his neck so she could put it around hers.

So many people came up to me and I don't even remember their faces or names. People I hadn't seen since my Kentucky childhood. There were people from my husband's workplace and family that had grown so much since I last saw them that I didn't even recognize who they were until they told me. I knew everyone who met Troy loved him (well, almost everyone) but I never knew he'd met so many people! They were sitting and standing everywhere!

Then there were all those flowers and mementos. Picture frames and angels of all shapes and sizes. I recall Troy's father Terry telling me that he had instructed his sister Vicki to keep an eye out for the flowers coming in and if Troy didn't get very many she was to go buy up everything the flower shop had. Oh, my goodness was that ever *not* necessary. They were continually delivered all day long and up until we left for the church the next day. I'd never seen so many arrangements at one funeral. My boy was truly loved by so many, many people.

It had been a long day and I was relieved when it was time to go home for the night. It was a somber three hour drive back up to Indiana. It was late enough that everyone was ready for bed by the time we arrived so I didn't have to talk much and talking was the last thing I felt like doing. The alarm woke me up, though I didn't sleep much. It was October 29, 2002, a day I didn't want to face, yet I knew I had to get out of that bed. Don't remember what anyone had to eat but I'm sure there was something; it was probably just cereal, toast and coffee. Funny how we can move along and do things when all we want to do is disappear into thin air and make everything go away.

The funeral home was once again full of people that morning. It wouldn't be long before we'd say our final good-byes and close the casket where something that resembled my handsome son laid ashen and motionless.

Troy's daughter, Jaidan, who was now three months and two days old, was crying her heart out. It was fitting for the scene. No one could soothe her. I took her for a walk, we changed her diaper, we made her a fresh bottle and still she screamed at the top of her lungs. It was time for the priest to give a little speech and still she cried. Shayna's mom, Dena, took her from me and sat a few rows back. It was difficult to concentrate on what the priest was saying with poor Jaidan crying so hard. He asked if anyone had anything they wanted to say about Troy. We only heard Jaidan. No one could bring themselves to go up so he concluded his speech and still Jaidan cried. They then played three songs that Terra and Shayna had requested and one of them was "Angel" by Sarah McLachlan. The same song in the movie Troy and Shayna had watched the night before the accident.

As soon as "Angel" started playing Jaidan went completely quiet. It was later that Dena was able to share with us one of many miraculous events that have taken place since Troy passed on. She said, "When the song started playing Jaidan immediately quieted down, laid back, spread her arms out, looked up above and gently moved one of her hands as if someone was tickling it lightly with a feather. She stayed that way until the song ended. She never cried again that day.

People milled around a little while longer. Some preacher from Illinois stopped by my seat and told me he'd visited with Troy in Illinois a couple times and thought he was a very special young man. I knew that already but it was nice of him to tell me. Danny and I finally got Terra up front to tell Troy good-bye. I was proud of her.

Then it was time. I was the first. I remember thinking later that I probably should've been last. I don't know how I ended up first. I don't think I even kissed him good-bye. I think I just brushed my hand over his suit. I don't remember but I knew already that it wasn't really him. Danny and I went to our vehicle and watched everyone file out the door. I can't remember if anyone rode with us to the church or if they rode with my sister. I only remember the little flag they put on the vehicle showing we were in a funeral procession. Watching a funeral go by now has a different meaning than it did before that day. I do remember looking back at all the cars following behind and being totally blown away all over again at how many people knew my Troy. The cars trailed back as far as I could see and they were still popping over the hill as we rounded the corner to drive the seven miles from Morganfield to Uniontown.

The service was held at St. Agnes. The same Catholic Church where I'd knelt practically every single day throughout my childhood. It's a beautiful big church with a choir up high in the back complete with a pipe organ. Funny how to this day I don't feel like I've been to church unless it's in a large one like that.

My family and Terry's family were all lined up in the front row. I never did like sitting in the front row. Troy's casket was in the aisle beside us and the priest had us stand up and position a white cloth over it. Then he handed a golden metal cross to me and motioned for me to lay it in the center. Fortunately, I didn't drop it and I had the strangest need to linger as if staying there would somehow not make it real. Afterwards, I found myself wishing I'd thought to bend down and kiss Jesus' feet to show him how much I appreciated him taking care of my son.

It seemed strange that there were two catholic priests serving at the mass instead of the usual one. I later found out that one was the regular priest and the other was one Troy had visited with a few times in another town. They'd talked and he thought Troy was a very special young man so when he heard about the accident he wanted to be there. There was another person that had words of praise for my son.

There was a period when we thought maybe Troy would join the priesthood. I remember one time when we were all back home for Christmas attending the mass at St. Agnes. Mom poked me and nodded toward Troy. He had his head down, his hands folded in his lap and was obviously deep in prayer or conversation with someone. Mom whispered, "I think he's going to be a priest." Well, he didn't quiet take that road but he always loved Jesus.

The priests both gave good speeches and I enjoyed hearing the kind words about my son. At one point in the catholic mass everyone shakes hands and says peace be with you or something similar and I remember Terry's brother, Wayne and his wife, coming all the way up to the front pew to give us hugs. I thought that was awful nice of them.

Then the final process was upon us too fast. We were walking out of the church behind the casket and watching them put it in a beautiful white hearse; that is if you can call a hearse beautiful.

The cemetery sits up on a hill just outside of town so it didn't take long to get there. Once again we were sitting in the front row, Terry on one side of me and Danny on the other.

As we were waiting for everyone to get situated I notice a worm crawling in the hole and nudged Terry to get it. He just looked at it so I leaned over, picked it up and threw it to the side. Of course, later I realized it probably wouldn't have lived long in the airtight vault anyway. It was just the idea of it.

One of the priests said a few more words then took the cross off I'd placed on so carefully and started to hand it to Terry. He told him to give it to his mother. That was special. I have it in my bedroom with a rose and wall hanging attached that Troy had given me shortly before the accident. It says:

Mother

God took the sunshine from the skies,

And made the love light in your eyes.

From honeyed flowers He took the dew

And made your tears, unselfish, true,

Upon a rock your faith He built,

With angel prayers your breath he filled,

And with His love made you divine,

But best of all He made you mine.

Then it was over. We walked away so they could put him in the cold, cold ground.

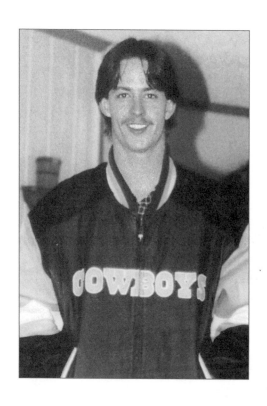

Make yourself familiar with the angels,
and behold them frequently in spirit;
for without being seen, they are present with you.

Saint Francis de Sales

He's Still Here

The next day Mom and Kimble, Janice and Audie went home and we were left alone. Not wanting to sleep in my own bed that night I went in the next room and laid down in the last bed Troy had slept in.

That was when the finality of it all hit me, that I would never be able to hold my first born child in my arms again, that I'd never see that special smile, feel his warm hug or hear him say, "I love you mom."

The shock of the last few days turned to tears and flowed like a river in a storm. I'd never experienced such anguish. Just when I didn't think I had anything left in me to come out I felt it! As soft and gentle as a feather it completely covered my body as if I was being wrapped in an Angels loving embrace. I fell into a deep, peaceful sleep.

As soon as I awoke the next morning I remembered the angel. There was no mistaking the soft, gentle being that lay on top of me to give me comfort the night before. I wanted to lay there as long as possible and keep the feeling. I wondered whether it was my guardian angel that I'd prayed to and depended on all my life to be there in times of trouble. From that day on there was no doubt in my mind that they really existed, however, I had no idea what impact one very special angel was going to have on not only my life, but the lives of my family.

From that day forward I believed God had heard and answered a mother's prayer and that my Troy was safe in his loving arms. I would be able to move forward, I'd found peace.

Although everyone tells me I look like my "Mamareney" and I know I do, I believe it's her husband, my granddaddy, Alvin Ruark, that I acquired my get up and go from. He worked on the farm from sun up till sundown until he was too old to get up and go. I suspect that's probably what kept him with us until he was 98 years old. Every time he would get anxious he'd have to get busy. I can remember when we'd go to visit. When it was time to pack up and leave he'd get busy as if it would somehow delay our leaving. He'd be fixing this and that. Sometimes I wondered if he purposely broke that old brass door handle going out the back door just so he could take it apart and put it back together again!

I too felt the need to stay busy after Troy was gone. Everyone was back to their regular routine so I decided to vacuum the floors. Pushing the cleaner into Troy's room I found myself talking to him. Well, Troy, I've heard our loved ones never really leave us so maybe you're still living in this room, huh?

As soon as the thought left my mind I looked down on the floor in front of the headboard on his bed and I saw it. It was a beautiful white feather.

Being skeptical, as we human beings are, I tore his bed apart. No, I didn't think there were any feather pillows on it nor was there a feather mattress. I looked at everything then decided there was only one place that feather could've come from. I promptly went out and bought a shadowbox frame to put it in. Between the "Angels" song at the funeral where Jaidan quieted down, the angel that held me in his bed that night and now this feather my skepticism had vanished. I knew an angel had left that feather for me. It would be the first of many to show up in times of need.

A friend of Shayna's had taken a recent picture of Shayna and Troy, put "In Memory of Troy Mills" on it and given us each copies at the funeral. I decided to crop it down and print it out for my family and friends. I'd spent most of the morning printing off several different sizes and laying them on the dining room table.

The dryer buzzing back in the utility room signaled it was time to take the clothes out. As I stepped back into the dining room I stopped in my tracks. I'd just received the greatest surprise and gift of my life.

There, lying on **that** table, next to all **those** pictures, was a single flower pulled out of the arrangement I'd received at his funeral. It was in that instant I felt my son was the angel that had shown up three times previously. I knew I was still loved.

Several days later I would be so thankful that I'd taken this picture as I would come to realize I was not the only person to receive a gift on this special day, November 6, 2002, exactly eleven days since Troy had been taken in the automobile accident.

That evening Terra came in shaken. She had been driving home on the state highway when a deer darted out from the edge of the road then suddenly stopped. She said the way it stopped is what amazed her; it was as if someone had blocked its path, not the normal way a deer would stop to run back. She felt sure it was Troy.

Talking to Shayna a few days later I found out that on the same day she had been driving on an icy road with Jaidan strapped in her car seat when the vehicle started to swerve. She knew they were going into the ditch. Suddenly the vehicle stopped spinning around on the ice. She couldn't believe it was also headed in the right direction. She felt Troy had saved them.

That same day Troy's friend Kara who he had been very close to was sitting in her bedroom on the bed thinking of him and smoking a cigarette. All of a sudden the cigarette went flying out of her fingers as if someone had knocked it out. She picked it up and again it flew out of her fingers. After the third time she finally realized what was going on and said, "Okay Troy, stop it!"

Trisha, his cousin, was born just a few days prior to him and she told me at the funeral he always felt more like her brother than her cousin. She loved him dearly. I found out that she too had a miracle on the eleventh day. She was standing by a cabinet when the football that Troy had given to her son fell off and hit her on the top of the head. The same football that had been in the same spot for years suddenly decided to jump off the cabinet. She knew Troy was still around.

I had learned as a Catholic that God's family is not separated upon death; I had further learned that one of the greatest saints who died at the young age of 24, Saint

Therese from Lisieux, France (known as the little flower) said that she would be able to help us more after she got to heaven. I knew my son wasn't a Saint Theresa but was God somehow allowing him to participate with the angels in the great heavenly mystery of consolation and help? I believe he is.

I'm sure there were probably many other miracles on that day which friends and relatives didn't recognize as such and after hearing all these stories I figured it must've been the day he came to give us a final good-bye but as time has moved on I've realized it wasn't a good-bye after all but messages to let us know he was still with us.

I went down to his dad's house in Kentucky so we could go through some of Troy's things. Terry was glowing as he opened the door for me to come in. It wasn't long before he was telling me of the most miraculous event of them all which took place for him on November 6, 2002. However, I feel it needs to be saved for a later chapter.

Angels and Feathers

I was about to find out that angels had been around Troy even before he took the ride of his life.

He had collected baseball and football cards for as long as I could remember and had several special ones of Troy Aikman. I planned to save everything for Jaidan, however, I thought of his friend Gary and how they hadn't gotten to attend that last football game together. I thought he might like to have one for a keepsake. At the funeral he'd asked me to keep in touch and I'd noticed that he hadn't signed the funeral book. I wanted his signature in there for Jaidan to see when she was grown.

I'd begun to drive down to Evansville one week-end each month where I'd meet Shayna and pick Jaidan up for a couple days then we'd meet again in the same place so she could go back home. Neither Shayna nor I wanted her to forget who her Mamatae was. We've been doing that now for almost eight years; however, since she started school the visits have become much less frequent.

Those trips have been full of special memories. I remember the time she was still just a few months old and we were having one of Indiana's rare blizzards. With the child restraint laws being what they are Jaidan had to be strapped in her car seat in the center position behind me facing the back seat. It was the only place I could reach her and still drive. As luck would have it she cried all the way home as soon as that pacifier would fall out of her mouth. She sure was attached to that thing. I can't even begin to guess the number of times I reached back, fished around for the "binky" and poked it back in her mouth on that long two hour drive! Whew, I'm so glad she's able to sit in the front seat and keep me company now.

As it happened I was scheduled to pick her up the week I realized Gary hadn't signed the book. I called to ask him if he'd like me to bring Jaidan over to see him explaining the book situation. He said he'd love to see how she'd grown and put his signature in Troy's book.

Terra went along for the ride. He was thrilled with the Troy Aikman football card and said he'd keep it forever. We had a nice visit with him, his son and his girlfriend and he enjoyed seeing his buddy's daughter. As we were talking he asked me if Troy had told me about the angels. Curiously, I looked at him and said, "No, what happened?"

He said, "Troy and I were standing outside in front of my trailer one night when he asked me if I saw those four angels standing out in the field across the street? I said, no, I don't see anything." So he said, yep, there are four angels standing out there watching us. Then Troy asked Gary if he died before he did would he come to the cemetery and pour a beer on his grave? He told him he would. Gary gave me a puzzled look and said, "We weren't even drinking a beer that night." I could tell by the look on his face that now he really believed it was possible the angels had been in the field watching and waiting for Troy. It was another confirmation for me that he was truly in heaven. I was glad we had taken Jaidan and the funeral book over for a visit.

Terry had called to ask if I could meet him in Henderson, Kentucky to pick out a stone for Troy's grave. We agreed on a time and I researched the different ones that were available on the internet. I had no idea there were so many different shapes, colors and ideas of what to put on one. It's just not something that a person usually thinks about until they have to. Terry had taken care of all the funeral expenses so I felt the need to pick up the tab on the stone. I wanted it to be extra special.

He was already there when I pulled in the driveway so he met me outside. He'd been in looking at the different books they had and just shook his head. There were so many choices. We walked around and he showed me a shape he thought he might like. He wanted a small vase on each side as the large ones on his mothers' stone were just too big. Other than that he was at a loss as to what we should put on it.

We went in and met with a nice, although rather timid gentleman. He had everything laid out on the table for us to look at. Terry seemed relieved when I pulled out my notes and showed them what I had in mind. The process actually went rather quickly from there. He didn't get the stone he first thought about as everything we decided to put on it wouldn't fit but I think he was happy with the results.

We decided on the paradise black granite which actually seems a strange name for a grave stone color. It actually consists of two stones side by side on top of a third. The front tall stone has an engraving of Jesus praying in the Garden of Gethsemane with the inscription, "do not stand at my grave and cry, I am not here, I did not die." The front of the smaller stone has a picture of Troy in a white shirt with that big smile on his face, two crosses, an engraved bible sketched with his official name, birth and death dates. Underneath it says, "To our Beloved Son. Always missed and never forgotten. Lord, we give you back our special angel Troy.

I drove down to see the finished stone and took some pictures after it was set up. He always called Jaidan honey so on the back of the small stone there is a photo of Troy in his Dallas Cowboys jacket with his familiar name beside it. Underneath is an inscription that says, "Loving Father of Jaidan "Honey" Arizona Mills" and under that it says, "To know him was to love him." The tall stone has a male angel engraved on it with the words, "His angel wings have taken him home to rest in Heaven with Jesus" at the bottom. I'm glad it's there for Jaidan to reflect on as she grows up in that town. The monument company did an excellent job.

The next day I downloaded the pictures from my camera and saw something I knew I hadn't taken. I enlarged the photo to the full computer screen so I could see what it was. I'd worn a t-shirt I'd bought at a craft fair with an angel painted on it. Seeing the picture gave me chills. I assumed Troy had taken the picture to show me he wasn't in that ground, that he was instead an angel in the sky above me. I wish I hadn't had my sunglasses hanging off my t-shirt; however, it was definitely another confirmation.

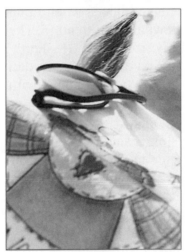

Things continued to happen on a regular basis. Some I took pictures of, others I didn't.

Danny got tired of hearing about them. He thought it was all silly superstition. We went on vacation to visit our daughter and grandchildren and I had gotten in the habit of asking God to send his angels to guard our home while we were away. Returning after a week we pulled in the driveway to find it covered in white feathers! I said to my husband, "Do you believe me now?" He didn't. I later drove up and down the highway looking for feathers to see if someone had taken a load of chickens by but the only feathers I could find were all in my driveway. I'd picked one up to keep and later my sister asked me why I didn't get a lot of them. Good question.

One day I picked it up to see what it smelled like and breathed in the fresh smell of rain and a new born baby mixed together. I assumed that's what heaven must smell like. Sometime later I found myself looking at the feather and wondering if anyone else would be able to smell what I did. Picking it up I took a big whiff. Dust! I guess the wonderful scent was meant for only me. It hasn't smelled like anything other than dust since I had that thought.

When you ask most people what they want for their children the majority will say just to be happy in whatever road they choose, or to be a doctor, lawyer or something in that order. You know what Troy wanted? That last visit when I took the picture of him holding his daughter he told me the most important thing he wanted for Jaidan was for her to get baptized in the Catholic Church. I never knew it meant that much to him.

In any case I took it upon myself to make sure that happened as it was his only wish.

The next year I arranged for both Jaidan and Terra's new daughter, DanTerrah, to be baptized together. While kneeling down during the mass I felt a poke as light as a feather to my right butt cheek. I smiled to myself thinking Troy must be pleased.

One time I was looking at his picture in the living room and when I turned to walk away with my hands behind my back I felt that same poke in the palm of my hand. Occasionally, I feel the slightest brush against my hair and there have been a few nights when I'd wake to an ever so gentle kiss on my lips.

One night I felt something different in my hair but I couldn't wake up enough to see what it was. The next morning I found the hair clip I'd had holding my hair up while I slept attached to the bear he and Terra had given me for my last birthday. It's still there.

Dream Visions & a Healing

I've been thinking of and procrastinating about this chapter for days. Although I am very proud of my heritage and a lot of what has happened centers around my faith, even though I was a "lost sheep" for years, I don't want this to be labeled as a catholic book. I believe that we are all children of God no matter what our religion or nationality is, just as long as we keep God in the first place. I believe that He has given us a free will to choose whether we work towards reuniting with Him in heaven or staying with the evil one.

I also don't want it to come across as a Danny bashing book, however, so much of the reason I have anguished and prayed from my heart in the past twelve years came about as a direct result of the things he said and did that I feel I have to include some of them so that the reader might understand the depth of my despair and the reason for some of my heartfelt prayers.

Most of all I want this book to be centered on the miraculous events that have mostly taken place since my son passed in the hopes that it can help people in this world. I especially want to give comfort to all the families, mostly mothers, which have lost children and loved ones. Whether they have gone to war and never returned or been taken by an accident or illness I want to give hope that they are still with you. More than anything I want to let everyone know that prayer works and we receive answers. I believe that if we believe completely, trust totally in God with our whole heart and soul the way Moses and Abraham did and give Him complete control He will take care of us and our loved ones. Even though we may not see it at certain times if we give Him everything in our lives He will arrange things in His way, in His own time and in the end when the end is really all that matters, it will be what is best for us. I know because it has happened to me.

Those things being stated I will continue to try painting a picture with words as my teacup Poodle and loyal friend, Tanar (short for Montana), sits in my lap keeping me company.

I have a small book of catholic daily devotions that I read a page from each day. It didn't surprise me when I turned to today's date, June 12, 2010, and realized it was the Roman Catholic feast of the "Immaculate Heart of Mary." It is the day that we celebrate the love in Mary's heart for her son Jesus and for God. It was just another confirmation for me that God is in control of this book and this special feast day encouraged me to write this book.

Many people throughout the world have different ideas of what dreams are about, the majority of them believing that they are a combination of our feelings and past experiences. I agree that is probably true with the largest majority of dreams. I've personally had a few nightmares but fortunately more dreams that I've enjoyed.

One that always stood out in my mind was the dream I had on several occasions of flying over top of the trees. It is the most marvelous feeling! On one particular occasion that dream took me a little farther and as I raced over the last tree in the row I looked down upon the most beautiful town I'd ever seen. So many people with smiling faces were standing around chatting with each other. I even saw my little sister Roxanne laughing out loud with a group of girls and holding a leash with her dog Chester at the end of it.

Then there were the colors! Like neon colors, so bright and beautiful.

Long after the dream, on a trip to Sedona, Arizona, I saw some paintings. The artist had captured those vibrant colors perfectly. They looked as if they'd come right out of my dream. In that instant I became convinced it must be what heaven is like. The beauty in this world pales in comparison, yet the scenic gifts we've been blessed with are so breath taking that it makes one wonder how there could possibly be something more beautiful. If my dream is any indication, then there is. Or, maybe it was just a combination of my feelings and past memories of seeing the kids playing with that bright neon foam they used to play with. However, I know beyond a shadow of a doubt that sometimes we are blessed with what I have chosen to label as a "dream/vision." Well, I thought I'd put that label on it. That is until I decided to type it into the search engine of my computer.

Imagine my surprise when several web addresses related to the subject popped up. Wikipedia, the free encyclopedia, states that a dream/vision is a literary genre, literary device or literary convention in which the narrator falls asleep and dreams. In the dream there is usually a guide, who imparts knowledge (often about religion or love) that the dreamer could not have learned otherwise. After waking the narrator usually resolves to share this knowledge with other people, which of course I have done and am doing. Well, that's pretty darned closed to what I experienced but I believe there was something more to it.

I believe there are times when we receive special messages during our sleeping hours either from our loved ones or heavenly beings. Of course if the message is from our loved one then it is also from a "heavenly being." I have had two of these. The first I've experienced signs that it was real; the second I choose to believe was also real.

One day in July of 1998 our doorbell rang. I was surprised to see our mailman, Rusty, standing there with a certified letter for me from the County Clerks office. After signing his little piece of paper he graciously presented me with it and told me to have a good day. Ha!

Talk about the shock of my life. Danny had filed for a divorce. I was almost floored. I knew we'd been having some problems but he'd never even hinted this! I was sitting at the little kitchen table by the window holding the papers in my hands when he came through the back door from work.

Still stunned I just looked at him and asked why in the world he'd done it? He looked back at me with tears in his eyes and said, "I don't know." That was it. No matter what I said or how hard I tried to get something out of him all he would say is, "I don't want to talk about it."

So there we were, the two of us walking around like zombies, him not speaking to me and me trying to figure out what the heck had happened. He seemed so upset at himself that he'd done it that I began to wonder if perhaps he'd gotten involved in something at work that he didn't want us associated with. It was almost like he was being forced to do it by someone else. Both our families were in shock as he had been such an exceptional husband and father until we moved to Indiana. His behavior was so strange that my family began to speculate that maybe he was being black mailed. They knew how much he had adored me and me him.

In any case, I didn't have a choice, although I didn't want to, I had to go counter file so I wouldn't lose everything. I couldn't believe it, when he received the notice he looked at me like I was crazy and asked why I'd counter filed!

Next thing you know I'm crying and begging him to cancel the darned thing. Yep, it was groveling at its worst. Finally, he told me he'd just done it to teach me a lesson, which he was going to do what he wanted, when he wanted and I was to stay out of his business. I wasn't allowed to ask about the women he worked with. He had planned only to shock me and cancel it but now that I had counter filed he wasn't sure what to do.

At that point I started praying that he would go through with cancelling it and with me afraid to open my mouth and him, well, I don't know what the heck he was doing but he began to go and come, sometimes for days or weeks at a time without telling me anything. In fact for the next five months he hardly spoke to me or the children and his temper became extremely short.

It was obvious he wasn't the man we knew and loved when he met Terra outside one night after she came home late and smacked her in the head several times. I wasn't out there but she told me later he had been smacking her head up against the garage door. She has some neurological problems now and I wonder if that night isn't at least partly to blame. He had become a person we didn't know and we all began to walk on eggshells. My prayers became more intense that he would forget about the other women and our family would be healed. I began talking extensively with our heavenly mother Mary and praying the catholic rosary on a daily basis. On one particular night I had a beautiful dream that gave me hope.

Danny, Terra and I were out taking a drive when all of a sudden Mary, the Mother of Jesus, came down out of the sky in front of us. Stopping the vehicle we just sat and stared at the most beautiful lady I'd ever seen smiling down. She was standing on a little white cloud with a bright white dress on. Over it she had a long blue cloak touching the cloud and a matching veil on her head. Her arms were down and her hands were turned up as if she was bestowing a grace on us. Completely surrounding her was a blue ribbon that matched her cloak and veil. It started and ended below her feet with one end lapping over the other. On each of the four corners, at the very top and on each side it was wrapped in a circle as it continued around her in one long continuous length. We just stared for the longest time. She was so beautiful and peaceful looking that I felt at peace.

Then I had the dumb idea to go home to get a camera so I could come back and take a picture of her.

In that instant she left, I woke up and heard the words, "something big is going to happen to the world." I thought, "Why did she tell me that - I wasn't praying for the world, I was praying for my family." I also remember wondering why Troy wasn't in the dream. It would be four years before I would finally realize she was telling me he wasn't going to be on this earth much longer. I finally understood why my son wasn't taking that ride with us.

She knew the kind of suffering I was preparing to go through because she went through it when her own son, Jesus, was crucified. I believe she wanted me to know that I wasn't alone, that she was there for me.

I began to tell everyone about the special dream emphasizing that pretty blue ribbon that circled around her. My aunt Betty asked me what the blue ribbon meant. I didn't know at the time.

Even though I thought the message was strange I had new hope that things were going to be o.k. and I felt a wonderful peace. In December, after five long months, we finally signed the papers to cancel the divorce and for a time, although different, things got better and we started to feel like a family again. Unfortunately, the peace was only temporary.

My mother had been expressing how much she'd like to visit our Aunt June in California so for her 65th birthday I surprised her with the trip. She flew from Minneapolis and I from Indianapolis to Las Vegas where we were met by Aunt June and my cousin Bobbi who is eight days older than me.

Vegas had sure changed in the past years. It's gotten so big that we spent most of our time just getting from one place to the next. I've never been much of a gambler, a few coins in a slot machine is all I can bear to lose. We walked into one particular casino where they had a huge machine in the entry way. To get a chance at the jackpot a person had to put in three one dollar coins. A lady was fishing through her purse for the coins when Bobbi decided to stand in line and give it a try. The lady felt she was holding up the line looking for her coins so she moved aside and gave Bobbi first chance. After dropping in a one dollar coin she reached for the handle.

Gees, I'm not much of a gambler but I couldn't believe she was only putting in **one** coin. I never take the chance of missing out on the jackpot by not dropping in the maximum number of coins. Oh, well, it was her choice. She pulled, the wheels began to spin round and round, one red seven stopped on the line, the second red seven stopped on the line, then, I couldn't believe it, a third red seven stopped! There were three red sevens in a row. She'd won the jackpot and she only had **one** coin in. There I was, depressed and devastated for her and she was jumping up and down like she'd just won the largest power ball payout of the year.

Then we looked at the poor lady standing in line. Oh, no! That poor woman probably never got over moving out of that line and missing out on that jackpot pull. However, Bobbi was ecstatic with her little win, we talked about it all the way to Tehachapi, California and it still provides a good laugh to this day. That was one well spent dollar.

We had a wonderful visit, mom had a 65th birthday complete with cake and ice cream that she would remember forever and I felt good about the decision to make the trip. Too soon it was time for them to drive us back to the Las Vegas airport.

I flew as far as Minneapolis with mom then on to Indianapolis where Danny picked me up Saturday evening. We stayed overnight and went out for a nice dinner then drove home the next day around noon. It was good to be back at home.

I started unpacking and he left to go check on the mine. It was a seven day a week job.

I checked the caller I.D. on the phone to see if I'd missed any important calls and noticed a lot of blocked calls. My stomach turned inside out and I started looking around to see if anything else was out of the ordinary. I walked into our bedroom.

Immediately I noticed the floral swag hanging on the wall above the headboard of our bed. The swag measures approximately 30" long by 12" tall. The flowers are almost exactly the same on each side with a bow tied in the middle. At least they had been, however, now the left side was missing quiet a bit of the arrangement. Obviously, it had been hit with something. I knew in that instant there had been someone else in our bed while I was in California. The floor behind the headboard next to the wall had been cleaned.

I was standing in the hallway in front of the desk which has four sharp corners when he came through the back door. He walked through the kitchen into the dining room and was standing about four feet away when I asked who the blocked calls on the phone were from.

He snapped, picked up the dining room chair and threw it across the room, then immediately swung his arm hitting me on the side of my head with the back of his hand. The force spun me around. My body slammed up against the wall then to the floor hitting my right shoulder on the sharp edge of the desk on the way down. As quick as it happened he was lying beside me saying how sorry he was and begging for forgiveness. I was stunned. Apparently I hadn't learned to keep my mouth shut.

He felt so bad; all he wanted to do was hold me. He ran a hot bath and we sat in it a long time that day, him in the back with me leaning back against him. My upper right arm and shoulder turned purple immediately in three different spots and was quickly getting sore. I took a couple of pain pills then we went to bed and just laid in quiet for the rest of the evening until we finally fell asleep.

The next day he went to work and without telling him I made a doctor's appointment in the next county. The doctor and nurse had the usual talk with me that I suppose they have with everyone that comes in the way I looked, gave me a card with an abuse hotline number on it and sad looks. I still couldn't believe I was even in a situation like this and threw the card away when I left. I don't know why she didn't x-ray the shoulder given the way it looked but considering I told her divorce was not an option I had the idea that she just didn't think much of a woman that would stay married in my situation. I understood that completely because before I was that woman I felt the same way!

Actually I did find myself thinking about divorce on many occasions after that but I'd made so many wrong choices in my life. I was afraid to make any kind of a move. So I just gave it all over to God and continued to pray more intensely. I focused on Mary and felt she was praying for me also.

It wasn't long before we were back to the old not speaking routine. Terra couldn't stand to be around and started hanging out at her boyfriend's more and Troy started mixing alcohol and drugs and spending his time in Kentucky. I think their hearts were as broken as mine if not more so.

I continued to draw strength from the dream and pondered the reason behind the blue ribbon. Then, on September 11, 2001 I was on a ladder listening to CNN Headline News on the TV and painting the trim blue that encircles my dining room, landing and sunken living room. They interrupted the regular scheduled programming to broadcast the news that the first plane had crashed into the World Trade Center, then the second. In the heart breaking days that followed it became apparent to me that Mary really had been there that night in the dream. I finally understood the reason for the blue ribbon. It was my confirmation that the dream was real. Chills ran down my spine yet my heart was almost bursting with joy. I felt so humbled. To know that I was important enough for her to appear to me like that turned my world around. Prayers and conversations with not only her but God and Jesus became more intense and personal. I had no doubt they heard and were near.

When Troy was taken in the automobile accident I even looked at that period in our lives as a special gift as I believed that had Danny not torn my heart out by filing for the divorce I wouldn't have been able to survive my son's passing.

This brings me to that second special dream. I missed Troy so much. It was almost unbearable. I thought of him constantly and wished I could hug him one last time. Then I got my wish in another dream vision. It seemed so real, I believe it was.

I was standing by the dining room table when I turned around and there he was.

So tall, so handsome, so - bright! He was dressed in the brightest, whitest jeans I'd ever seen, a neon pink polo shirt with neon pink socks to match and a pair of bright white tennis shoes. Of course he had that big smile on his face. My heart leaped into my throat as he started walking toward me and I wondered if I'd be able to feel his hug. Apparently I knew he was already in heaven. I didn't have to wonder long. He came right over and put his arms around me in a big wonderful embrace. I held on for dear life and in the next instant I heard, "I have to go now mom." I heard it the same way I heard Mary that morning. Not by human voice but by what I can only think of as mental telepathy. He let go and walked passed me. I turned immediately but he was already gone. The feeling of that moment has never left and I truly believe he came back in human form just long enough to give me that one last hug and to let me know my prayers for him had been answered. I will always be thankful to God for allowing us that final human moment.

Something else I've come to realize the past ten years or so. The more we thank God for His blessings instead of complaining about our woes, the more blessings He bestows on us. I have developed a favorite prayer I say everyday now, sometimes more. "Thank you God for all your blessings, big and small, I appreciate them all." It amazes me how something so simple can make me feel so good.

The weekly bulletin of the church I was attending advertised a senior citizen bus tour for Saint-Mary-of-the-Woods College in Terre Haute, Indiana and the annual Madison County covered bridge festival. Although I'd been to the festival several times I hadn't yet made it to the college area I'd heard so much about and always wanted to visit.

Founded in 1840 by Saint Mother Theodore Guerin and the Sisters of Providence, Saint-Mary-of the-Woods College is the oldest Catholic liberal arts college for women in the United States. I called the church office and told them that although I wasn't a senior citizen yet I'd sure like to tag along for the tour. The lady I was talking to chuckled and agreed to let me go. I could hardly wait for the day.

As soon as the bus pulled into the long driveway of the campus I was mesmerized. I felt like I'd been there before although I knew I hadn't. The church on the grounds, The Immaculate Conception, was completed in 1907. I walked into the sanctuary and caught my breath. There, high above the altar was Mary with her arms and hands stretched out just like they had been in my dream. I felt as if I was home.

We enjoyed a marvelous brunch in the O'Shaughnessy dining room, built in 1921; it's all painted in ivory with magnificent columns and beautiful architecture. We visited the little shell chapel, the cemetery, the alpacas that they raise and the grotto where once again I felt drawn.

The grotto is a replica of the original grotto in Lourdes, France where Mary appeared to a 14 year old peasant girl named Bernadette Soubirous on a total of 18 occasions starting on February 11, 1858. She directed her to a dry spot of ground and instructed her to start digging with her hands. Soon water started trickling up and has ever since sprung forth 27,000 gallons per week. Today Lourdes has a population of around 15,000. An estimated 200 million people have visited the shrine since 1860 and many have had miraculous healings.

From that day on I have attended the church at St. Mary of the Woods. They have a wonderful priest, Father Dan, whose sermons always seem to answer a question I have milling around in my head and the Sisters of Providence nuns who always make me feel welcomed. I've made regular visits to the grotto where a statue of Mary stands in the rocks. I visit and talk to her asking her to pray for me and my family.

On February 11, 2008 France celebrated the 150th anniversary of the appearance of Mary at the Lourdes grotto with 45,000 people in attendance. Eight days before, on February 3, 2008, Danny and I were seated in the cracker barrel restaurant waiting for our lunch to be served. As always, I say a blessing to myself in restaurants before the meal. As I started that blessing, in the middle of my back, on the left side, I felt a wonderful sensation travel from the middle point up along my spine to the top of my neck.

Previously I'd had an MRI showing two bulging discs on the left side of my neck. Since that day I've had no pain on the left side of my spine. Once again I knew Mary was praying for me and God was listening.

Animals and Children

I've heard it said that animals can see another world that most of us can't and that children up to the age of two or three can also. Considering what I've seen since Troy's passing I have to agree with that statement.

Animals are never able to reason that an angel or spirit might not exist whereas babies and toddlers wouldn't understand if we told them they didn't. They only know what they see and feel.

Perhaps you have read or heard some of the stories about toddlers that have fallen out of high buildings only to land without a scratch. The only explanation was that something or someone cushioned their fall. Most adults tend to try and rationalize this when actually it's as simple as being helped by someone who loves us. Someone, probably several someone's who are around us all the time; even though we can't see them, they are there.

I've seen it evidenced by my dog Tanar. He will turn twelve years old this year on July 18, 2010. He's been around long enough that he pretty well knows my routines as well as I know his. He follows almost all my steps. My friend Dennis once said, "If you put tap shoes on him you'll have a tap dance down the hallway!" It's a comforting sound to hear the little pitter patter of his nails tapping the floor as he follows me back and forth. I can tell when he is looking at someone that I can't see and he does it on a regular basis. Watching him can sometimes be pretty entertaining.

He always sits on the little rug in the bathroom waiting for me and will occasionally leave just long enough to run back to the utility room to his training pad then back to me he runs. A couple of days ago he started out the door then stopped, looked up, backed up and whined. It was pretty obvious his exit was being blocked. He sat back down on the rug and I just smiled. These little moments have become part of my every day life and I've come to expect them. I'd be disappointed if they suddenly stopped.

Several times this past couple of years he and I have been sitting in the living room, with me either watching TV or reading. He's either sitting on my lap or lying on his dog bed in front of me. All of a sudden he'll yelp and jump up off that bed like he's been shot! It's the funniest sight. He turns around immediately to see who poked or pinched him and I just smile to myself. Sometimes I'll say, "Hello Troy." Its obvious Tanar and I are not alone.

Occasionally he'll run back and forth as if someone is playing with him. Not like we see dogs usually run back and forth playing. This is different. He'll take off running, stop, look up as if someone is there and take off again and again until he's completely worn out.

I feel dogs are one of God's most special gifts to us. There is nothing else on this earth that gives us perfect, unconditional love. Maybe that's why dog spelled backwards is God.

It would be nice to see what Tanar and the babies see. Since I had Jaidan visiting me regularly and Terra lived with us until DanTerrah was three years old I had the special blessing of watching them grow and interact.

I wonder how many times parents have brushed off their child's "imaginary" friends when in reality that friend was not imaginary at all. I can remember lying Jaidan on her daddy's bed to change her diaper when she was just a few months old and seeing her eyes dance as she reached up above her and giggled at the angel she was playing with.

Many times Terra and I would hear DanTerrah laughing and giggling in her bed as if someone was playing with her or she'd crawl up and down the hallway as fast as she could go always glancing behind to see if "whoever" was about to catch up.

Just before Jaidan turned two I brought her up here to celebrate her birthday with some of my family members; they were in for a vacation. The adults were standing in the kitchen talking when I felt this little tap, tap on my leg from behind. Turning around, I caught my breath. There was Jaidan, not tall enough to reach past the edge of the dining room table, holding up a flower for me (the same exact kind of flower that had been pulled out of the arrangement and laid on the table the day I was printing out Troy's pictures). There was no possible way Jaidan could have reached up into that arrangement in the middle of that oval table and pulled that flower out and all the heavy chairs were scooted all the way in. Where did it come from? The only possible explanation we could come up with is her daddy gave it to her to give to his mom. It has been sitting on top of the picture frame I put the first feather in ever since that day.

I like to sit at that dining room table as it has a huge picture window that looks out on the state highway running in front of my home. There's a steady flow of traffic and about halfway between this home and that highway I have what I call my "bird tree." It's just a tall maple with bird feeders under it on metal hooks. No matter how bad I might be feeling, if I go sit at that table and watch the many species of birds visiting the feeders, my spirits will lift. Birds are another one of God's greatest gifts.

DanTerrah and I were sitting there on a day I will never forget. She was learning how to arrange her alphabets on a little board with individual slots in it for each letter and doing a pretty darned good job. Not quite two years old yet she wasn't talking a whole lot but could put some words together. I was watching her intently when all of a sudden she stopped and looked above that flower arrangement (yes, the same one). It was obvious she was listening to someone talking to her. She held that look on her face for several seconds then she looked at me and said, "Man won't hurt you." I said, "What did you say?" Once again she repeated, "Man won't hurt you." I said, "Where did the man go?" She raised her arm, turned and pointed out the dining room window. It seemed to be the most natural thing for her but it had the most special heartwarming effect on me. Just thinking about it again makes me feel like bursting out in tears of joy.

I have come to realize that the more open we are to such things, the more we believe and most especially the more we "trust" the more we will receive. Just like the day the angel Gabriel appeared to Mary and asked her to be the mother of the son of God. She never doubted he was real. If we can remove that doubt from our brains, I believe that we too can receive these wonderful visits.

My mother's faith is as solid as a rock but it took a lot of miracles before she reached that point where she could really feel they are so close to us. I think I finally convinced her. She called all excited a couple weeks ago and said she'd had a miracle. For years she's had a shelf full of knick knacks that have never moved. On this day her angel statue was moved to the edge. She was ecstatic. Although I refer to them as miracles I've come to believe they are just part of all our normal everyday lives.

Troy and Terra gave me a little pillow on my last birthday before the accident. It says, "Miracles happen to those who believe." Yes, if we only "believe" and "trust" we will receive.

Jaidan, Tanar, DanTerrah

Terra and Troy

Miraculous Flowers

Have you ever thought about how different our world would be without flowers? We use them for everything from welcoming a new born baby into the world to saying good-bye to a friend or loved one and everything in between. We plant, pick, dry and press them. Some say they've even received flowers from a recently deceased relative. I think I have.

I've received so many special flowers since Troy passed that I've lost count. Some I have pictures of, many I don't. Some might reason they could be explained away as the wind or birds' dropping a seed and it seems we always look for a reasonable explanation when it happens. However, I know that some are brought by angels.

Like the cannas that sprouted in front of my kitchen window last year. They grow from bulbs which have to be planted, not from seeds.

Christmas, 2008, it was the first one I'd spent alone in my 55 years. I figured it would just be another day. As soon as I opened my window blinds that morning my eyes were drawn to a spot of red in the front yard. What the heck is that I wondered? Is it a flower? Curiosity soon won over and I quickly slipped out the front door and down the slope of the front lawn to investigate. Well, I'll be darned; it was just one single artificial red poinsettia. Had it blown out of someone's vehicle? Maybe I wasn't alone after all. I had a smile in my heart all day after receiving that special Christmas gift.

The first "special" flower I can remember was a rose. I have twenty four red ground cover roses planted out in front of my home lining the sidewalk and patio to the entry door. One year, and only one year after he was gone, one, and only one of those red rose bushes bloomed with half pink blossoms that were larger than the red ones.

I couldn't imagine how that could've happened so I took a picture; emailed it to the large rose producer I'd bought the bushes from and asked them for an explanation. When they replied that it was impossible because the roses were not produced from grafted plants I had my first inclination that maybe, just maybe Troy had sent it to me.

Since that first rose I've had many I can put in that category. Like the red impatient that sprouted by the back door where I always spray roundup to keep the weeds away from the edge of the house. I will forever regret fussing at Jaidan when she spotted it and quickly plucked it for me before I could stop her. I gave her a big hug and tried to explain how it upset me as I felt maybe her daddy had planted it there.

Now when there are special flowers around I explain to the grandkids which ones they can and can't pick. I love working outside. Planting flowers quickly dissolves my stress away so I have a lot of flower beds for them to enjoy and pick from.

I started one at the end of the driveway where I planted white petunias around the telephone pole. A beautiful red rose moss showed up at the top on the side where the driveway is. Every time I went somewhere I felt good seeing it as I exited and entered the driveway. I was so delighted and thankful.

Then petunias started sprouting up in the gravel at the entry to my garage. I'm greeted with lovely flowers growing in my rocks each time I pull in and out of my parking spot. Although I have to spend a large amount of time watering my other flowers, especially during the hot dry dog days of summer I've never watered the petunias growing in the rocks. In fact I've never done anything other than enjoy their presence. They are there every year.

This past winter, 2009, was a peaceful time for me. No more anxiety attacks. However, by March I was tiring of the cold chore of servicing the hot tub. Especially since I hadn't used it much since it had gotten so cold.

As I stepped out the back door bundled up in warm clothes, a coat and cotton stuffed in my left ear so I wouldn't get an ear ache I found myself where I don't go too often. On the pity pot! I was sure wishing I didn't have to deal with the hot tub that day.

Then I saw it. What I refer to as a "monkey flower". My daughter, Terra, had given me a hanging basket of them the past summer and I'd smiled every time I caught a glimpse of them smiling back at me from their spot on the patio. I couldn't believe it! One had sprouted right beside the hot tub steps in the crack between the four by four and the bricks and there it was smiling up at me.

Talk about how quick a person's spirits can lift! That was the end of the pity pot day for me. I looked all around the back yard and couldn't find another one sprouting anywhere that cold March day. Knowing that the viola is a cold weather plant it was possible a seed could've blown over from Terra's arrangement that past summer and sprouted but finding it looking up at me at just the right moment in the perfect spot was nothing less than a miracle. I felt warm the rest of the day.

Just when I felt I'd had pretty much every flower surprise I could experience the ultimate one showed up.

DanTerrah was visiting the summer of 2008. She and I were sitting in my favorite spot on the property. A three seat swing in the back yard between the patio and the rose garden. From that spot I can watch the traffic on the highway and see my garden along with a lot of the flower beds. Birds, butterflies, bees, fireflies, dragonflies, squirrels, deer, coyotes, rabbits, raccoons, skunks, opossums, a chipmunk and an occasional snake show up to entertain me.

The rose garden is so named because my mother loves roses, as do I, so I made three of them the focal point in the front of the 15 X 15 foot area. Along with the roses for mom I planted the favorites of Terra and my sisters. Terra loves columbines, Janice favors the Stella De Oro lily and Roxanne loves any and all daisies. I've added some clematis and a few other flowers to balance out the area with a red double tropical hibiscus in the center which I move in and out of the building each spring and fall. In the front corner is a small angel statue mom gave me and a plaque I found at a flower shop that says, "Expect miracles." It has become my favorite garden.

We were gently swinging back and forth and I was studying the rose garden and thinking of the bright yellow lily I'd seen in someone's yard recently. I was wondering what kind it was and wishing I had one for the rose garden when five year old DanTerrah asked me if we could take a ride in the mule. Of course we could.

I enjoyed the Kawasaki mule as much as Jaidan and DanTerrah did so we frequently took rides around the property which is almost 12 acres. I'd slow down or stop along the way so they could reach out and pick some of the wild flowers growing in different spots. They love to sit in the driver's seat while I control the gas and brake pedals.

There's a small hill at the back edge of the yard we always drive up on and across. Behind that hill is a field full of weeds and small trees and bushes. We slowly drove up the short slope to the top of the hill and came to a dead stop. Tears welled up in my eyes. DanTerrah looked at me. There, in that field, not two feet from where we were stopped was the most beautiful bright yellow lily I'd ever seen, just like the one I'd seen in that persons yard.

In the 12 years I have lived here I had never seen a lily like that growing anywhere except for the one I saw that day in the yard. There was no doubt in my mind that heaven had allowed Troy to give me this very special miracle.

I immediately turned the mule off, jumped out, grabbed the shovel in the back and dug it up. It had three small dirt encrusted bulbs attached to its roots. I told DanTerrah it was our miracle flower from her uncle Troy and we were going to plant it in the rose garden. She thought that was okay, so off we went.

I divided the three bulbs. We planted the largest on one side of the Stella De Oro lily and the two smaller ones on the other side and thanked God for his most special blessing. Not only did they live but this year, just two years after DanTerrah and I found it growing in that field, both plants are flourishing and I have another reason to sit in my swing, smile and be thankful. I saw a lily at the flower shop last week that looked just like them. It is called, "Happy Returns." I'm not surprised.

Mary's Garden

I think there must be an unwritten law somewhere that says it's okay to throw trash out of your vehicle when you're in the country. What do people think that it just magically disappears if they're out of the city limits? I almost always have some in my yard. I believe that if you look hard enough you will usually find something good in the bad so on the up side of this little problem I'm thankful for the free exercise I get gathering up the unsightly nuisance.

It was May 1, 2008, and I'd had a steady stream of little miracles that year, more than usual it seemed. Every other day or so I was relaying something new to mom and anyone else in the family I happened to have a phone conversation with. Really didn't surprise me. The year ended in the number 8. No beginning and no ending. Just like God. I'd become particularly fond of that number and it seemed to pop up on a regular basis.

May 1st always had a special meaning to me also. It was the start of Mary's month.

She is the woman who God picked out from all the others on earth to give birth to his son. For that reason catholics dedicate and name May for the month of Mary.

Every year while I was attending St. Agnes grade school we had a procession of all the kids, nuns and priest to the statue of Mary where we would place a crown of flowers on her head. As we marched down the sidewalk we sang, "O Mary, we crown thee with blossoms today, Queen of the Angels, Queen of the May." The title of the song is, "Bring flowers of the fairest." It was always a special day.

Therefore, it seemed appropriate that I should go outside to clean up my Mary's garden and plant some flowers for her. However, first I needed to pick up all that trash littering my yard! It didn't take too awful long, and then I turned my attention to the garden.

The spot at the edge of my driveway contained only grass when we moved in fourteen years ago. It looked like a perfect home for a statue of Mary. I took my friend Becky on a treasure hunt of sorts. We located the perfect concrete Mary, managed to load her up, bring her home and deposit her in the appropriate spot. Then I gathered up some of the stones that were left over from the construction of the short stone wall bordering the driveway on each side and placed them in front of the statue so they butted up against the stone wall on each side. Finally, I added flowers and mulch.

I was happy with the end result. I've varied the flowers over the years and have noticed that, although the stones in front came from the same lot as the ones in the back, they seem to get whiter each year.

I gathered up the petunias, daisies, zinnias and calla lily along with the trowel and my kneeling pad. It hadn't rained for awhile so the ground was hard. I found myself wishing, once again, that I'd amended the clay soil a little better when I put the garden in.

As I was digging and planting I was talking to Mary confident that she was listening. It's nice to know that our heavenly mother is always available when we want to talk about something. It's nice to know we have a go between so to speak, who is always encouraging us on the path to God. I always ask her to pray for me, my family and friends and I'm sure she does.

Well, okay, I was finished. I said, "There you go Mary, I hope you like them." Then I heard a slight rustle. Looking off to my left I saw a plastic bag and wondered where the heck it had come from since I'd just picked up all the trash in the yard and we were quiet a ways back from the highway.

I stood up, walked over, picked it up, looked at it, smiled to myself, and then said, "Thank you Mary, I'm glad you like them." The plastic bag is in a frame in my hallway.

The Wind and Birds

He makes winds his messengers ... Psalms 104:4

The radio was reporting a wind advisory with 70 mile per hour gusts for the day and they had hit the nail on the head this time. I had to hang onto the steering wheel to keep from being blown off the highway as I drove home from church.

As usual I pulled into the driveway and pushed the garage door opener only this time nothing happened. Obviously the wind had knocked out the electricity. No telling how long it would be off this time. Danny was working in South America so he wouldn't be inside to open it for me.

There was nothing to do but battle the gusts and go open the back door. It was a chore just to get the vehicle door open and closed. As I was walking around to the back of the house I was watching the trees blowing in the wind. Just as my eye traveled to the small hill, then to the woods on the left, I noticed something coming out of them. It was a balloon!

Not just any old balloon, a huge Mylar balloon. It was probably two or three foot tall by a foot or so wide. It danced along the hill then angled toward me, close enough to see but too far out to catch. Well, I'll be darned. It was silver with a big pink heart in the middle that said, "I Love

You." Well how about that. What a wonderful day. What a marvelous gift. What perfect timing! I watched it float off toward the town of Dugger until it was completely out of sight, another special gift from heaven.

It wasn't the first Sunday I'd come home from church to a special gift. I love the birds. I have several species at my feeders and just recently I had a couple owls show up. I noticed them sitting on my dog fence in the back yard one morning last week, in broad daylight! Thinking this was unusual I emailed an owl expert with a picture of them. She wrote back that they were probably a couple curious kids and although their parents would stay in the area they'd probably move on in the fall.

I arrived home one Sunday to see a pigeon on top of my house; I wasn't too surprised. I hadn't seen any in this area but figured there probably were some around here since it's so much like the area where I grew up in Kentucky. Uniontown was covered with pigeons. So many, that every year around voting time the men would gather downtown with their guns to shoot them off the top of the bank and other buildings. After they were gutted and cleaned they would be added to big black kettles along with several other kinds of wild and tame meats and a few vegetables. Then the men would spend hours outside stirring this mixture over a hot fire so everyone in town would be able to enjoy steaming hot bowls of "burgoo" on voting day. It was a tradition and favorite time of year.

I pulled the car in the garage then walked around to the front of the house. Surprisingly, the pigeon just looked at me curiously. Not only did it not fly off, it flew down to the patio and landed beside my feet. Oh, my goodness, someone must've lost their tame pigeon.

I went inside and grabbed a handful of my wild bird seed. Although it was back up on the roof when I came around the corner it wasted no time flying back down to the patio when I scattered the bird seed. This was amazing and I took off to get my camera.

I named her "Matilda." The next morning I went outside and didn't see her. Within moments she was beside me. For over a week she followed me around like a puppy dog. Didn't matter if I was in the front yard or the back yard, she was either beside me or up on the roof of the house watching. It was the neatest thing. Then she was gone.

Although we'd always had robins around from spring through fall they became extra special to me just a few days after we'd buried Troy.

I awoke just before daybreak one morning, walked into his room and looked out the window. I could hear a bird singing so beautifully but I couldn't see it. I was mesmerized; it was the most beautiful melody. I was frozen in the spot when finally the sun peeked up just far enough for me to see it. Perched right on top of the head of a concrete angel I have sitting under two pine trees was a robin. It continued singing for the longest time and although I felt it was a message just for me, that morning, I had no idea what a special impact robins were going to have on my life.

Danny had continued to grow more and more irritable. One day he was sitting in the hot tub so I decided to join him. As I climbed in I said something that apparently he didn't like because he screamed at me. My heart jumped to my throat and I became sick to my stomach.

Immediately, robins started flying into the maple tree that is about ten yards from the hot tub. There were twenty, thirty, maybe even forty or more! They started singing that beautiful melody I'd heard coming from the robin on top of the angel the morning I looked out Troy's window. It was the most beautiful sound I'd ever heard. I looked at them, then at Danny who had his head down sulking, then back to them. For what seemed like several minutes I looked back and forth from them to him. He never looked up. How could he not hear them? They were singing so loud! Then, just as quick as they'd landed they flew away. Apparently it had just been a gift for me.

Not long after that we were sitting out back in the swing. Previously, I'd asked our doctor if the changes in Danny could be caused by his medications. She simply said, "No, he just doesn't love you anymore." I'd become accustomed to talking to God about my situation. That particular day was no different.

All of a sudden a Canadian goose landed out in the field. I love the geese and have enjoyed listening to them squawk as they fly over to the lake behind the woods. I'd never seen one land on our property but there it was. Just as I was pondering whether I should stay here or give up and leave. I said to myself, well actually to God, "Okay God, I'm going to walk out to that goose - if it stays I will and if it leaves I will."

Can you believe I walked up within a few feet of that wild goose and it just looked at me? So I said something silly to that gorgeous bird then turned around and walked back to the swing. It wasn't long before that goose took flight, circled the lot and flew out to the lake. Okay God, thank you. I haven't seen one on this property since.

The summer before Troy passed I was at the computer when he came in from the garage smiling from ear to ear. I said, "What have you got in your hands." "A hummingbird, he beamed, I picked it off the inside garage wall." Neither one of us could figure out how it got in there but it was a special treat. Turned out he wouldn't be the only one to hold a hummingbird.

I have a feeder hanging just outside my kitchen window where we are well entertained during the summer months. Jaidan and I were sitting at the little kitchen table eating one sunny day.

All of a sudden she said, "Look Mamatae!" There was a little hummingbird caught in a spider web in the bottom corner on the outside of the window right where she was sitting. I told her that her daddy had sent her a special gift from heaven then we went outside and gathered the little fellow up. Perfect timing! This time I took a good picture.

Trees

Have you ever seen one lonely tree out in the middle of a field and wondered why there was only one? Put a herd of cattle in there on a hot day and you'll have your answer. When farmers clear a field for planting they'll leave one tree for the livestock. Where would they be if they didn't have that shade tree? Nothing compares to sitting under a shade tree on a blistering hot day, feeling a gentle breeze and watching the leaves sway ever so gently. Yes, God did a good thing when he invented trees.

I'll never forget the tree that saved my life, my sister Janice's and my brother Joe's at granddaddy's farm one summer. Billy and Roxanne weren't with us that day. There were several ponds on the property; some for swimming in and others for fishing. All were used to water the livestock. I'd recently caught a huge snapping turtle by the tail with my fishing pole in what we called the "back pond" since it was at the back edge of the property. As soon as that turtle was able to dig all four of his feet into dry ground he was off my hook and back in that pond. I was probably fifteen or sixteen years old.

My siblings and I were discussing that event one day when we decided to go catch that darned turtle! Off we went, fishing poles slung over our shoulders. When we arrived at the back fence we noticed the cattle were giving us suspicious looks so I told Joe to wait while Janice and I walked out to the pond so we could see what they would do.

She and I climbed over the fence and were about half way between it and the pond when the bull came after us with a herd of cattle right behind him! That tree hanging out over that pond looked like a much quicker and safer escape than making it back to that fence did so off we ran. About the same time Joe took off across the field to find Granddaddy. Here they came in his old Ford farm truck to rescue us. Yes, thank God for trees. Janice and I were hanging over top of the pond as we had both climbed about as far out on the limbs as we dared to without risking the chance the limb would break and we'd end up in the pond. Every time the three of us get together we laugh at how Joe and I blamed Janice because she had a red shirt on that day.

I have a special tree at the back of my property also. The Christmas after Troy passed I didn't feel like getting a big tree and putting up the usual decorations, however, I wanted to do something for Terra. We decided to purchase a small blue spruce that we could decorate with Troy's Dallas Cowboy memorabilia, and then plant it outside in his memory after the holidays.

That tree has flourished since we put it in the ground but it's what we've received from it that is so special. Troy knew how much I liked blackberries so one year he went out and picked a tub full of wild ones so I could make us a blackberry cobbler. The very first summer after we planted the blue spruce a wild blackberry bush wound up on it and gave us three blackberries. There was one for me, one for Danny and one for Terra. The thing that amazed us most - the other wild blackberries growing on our property were just barely turning pink and were only about ½ the size of Troy's blackberries. It had large blackberries on it ever since. In fact I stopped my mower and picked a few just this past week and popped them in my mouth. They were so sweet.

When I moved from Montana to Indiana my dear friend Deb asked me to plant a peach tree so watching it grow would bring back memories of her. As if I could ever forget our escapades on the ambulance. She is a silly girl. I decided to plant two. Hers grew, mine didn't. From the time it was mature enough it produced such an abundance of fruit every year that the limbs would touch the ground with their heavy weight, except for two.

The first was in 2005 when DanTerrah was two years old. There was only one lone peach on the entire tree way up high. We watched it ripen, afraid it would fall off the tree before it was ready or the birds would get it. Luckily it survived. We were in awe at the size of the thing. We had never seen such a large peach! DanTerrah proudly held it so I could take a picture before we cut it open. If the size astounded us it was nothing compared to the taste. It was the sweetest, juiciest peach ever. Surely it was a miracle.

The next year the tree was once again loaded with our normal amount of normal sized peaches. There was plenty for us to eat, cook and freeze. We have so many that I get tired of peeling, pitting and slicing them by the end of the season. Just when I thought the peach tree was back on track 2007 rolled around. We looked and looked but there was not a single peach that year and we couldn't for the life of us figure out why? Still, we kept looking as if that act alone would produce the peaches we so enjoyed. The ones

I'd frozen were long gone and I really didn't want to have to buy any from the market but that's exactly what I ended up doing.

Jaidan was up visiting and she and I were sitting out on the back swing. Looking over at the peach tree she said, "Mamatae, where are all the peaches?" I said, "Honey if you can find a peach on that tree it will be a miracle, it just doesn't have any this year." Disappointed, she got up and walked over to the tree and hollered, "Mamatae - I see a peach!"

Danny and I both went running over to the tree and sure enough, there it was, a single, luscious peach way up high. Danny said, "I just looked at that tree yesterday and there was no peaches on it." I said, I know, I didn't see any either but obviously it's there now. Must be a miracle for Jaidan from her daddy and I ran into the house to get the camera. Don't know why I didn't take one of her holding it. We've had an abundance of peaches ever since.

DanTerrah

Peach tree loaded

Same peach tree with one peach

Just This Morning

The ground on this property is pretty rough in places and the recent occupation of ground moles have added to the problem. I used to have a beautiful golden retriever named Kaedo who was the best mole dog I've ever seen. He'd walk over to a spot, listen, and then start digging with the fury of a heavy weight boxer going for the knock out. Sure enough, nine times out of ten he'd produce a mole.

Occasionally, he'd bring it over and deposit the stunned varmint at my feet but most of the time he'd just start batting it around like a ball. After a few minutes (I figured he deserved a little entertainment for all his hard work) I'd grab the shovel so I could put the thing out of its misery. It took about four years for Kaedo to completely eradicate the mole problem. I lost my best friend to cancer two and a half years ago in December of 2007 and the moles have just recently made their way back into my yard.

Between their tunneled hills and all the holes it's a chore just to keep everything from jarring out of place while I'm riding the mower. After more than seven hours battling the bumps in the hot 87 degree temperature yesterday I was beat and not surprised to see the clock said it was after nine a.m. when I finally rolled out of bed this morning.

Flipping the switch on the coffee maker as I entered the kitchen I noticed Tanar heading towards me anxious for the few cheerios he starts his day off with. I fixed my cereal, poured a glass of water, grabbed my handful of vitamins and another few dry cheerios for Tanar, and then opened the kitchen and dining room window blinds before I plopped down at the table. Tanar took his usual spot on the floor beside me awaiting the first cheerio drop.

Immediately, I noticed the vehicles driving slowly and looking toward the house. About the time I started wondering what the heck they were looking at something showed up at the side of the highway. It was a deer, a baby deer! The poor thing didn't seem to have a mom or dad around and was trying to cross that busy highway. It frantically took off, back towards my house. I jumped up and ran over to the patio doors thinking it was probably headed toward the woods on the west side.

Pulling the blinds open I caught my breath. There it was, not three or four feet away. The prettiest little fawn I'd ever seen covered in white spots. In a matter of a few seconds it bolted toward the woods. I flew outside!

It was nowhere to be seen and my joy turned to sadness at the thought of it being so young and all alone. There was nothing to do but go on back in the house. Poor Tanar had a look of what the heck is going on - we didn't finish our cereal. I dropped a couple more pieces on the floor for him and was about half way through my bowl when the fawn came waltzing into view.

Grabbing my camera, I snapped a couple pictures from the inside then went back out. Rounding the corner of the house I started making a noise I thought might keep its attention. It worked. The pretty little "bambi" looked right at me and I snapped another picture before coming in to call the conservation officer. It seems they let nature take its course so the fawn was on its own. Luckily, it made it across the highway without being splattered into buzzard meat. What a special morning.

Tanar and I finished our breakfast and I was thinking of all the wonderful things that had happened to me since

Troy's passing. Maybe, just maybe this was another special gift from God.

Just like Kaedo. He was a special gift. He actually belonged to my daughter but as so often happens to parents with their children's pets, he ended up with me. I've had several dogs in my lifetime but he was my favorite.

He showed up at a time in my life when I really needed a friend. He was probably only a year old when he heard the grandchildren of my neighbor across the street playing ball. Anxious to join in the laughter, he took off across that busy highway before I had time to stop him. I marched across the street, grabbed his collar and led him to his outdoor pen not saying a word. I didn't scold him; I just put him in his pen, closed and latched the gate. Then, for the next three days I took food and water out to the pen and sat it inside without speaking to or petting him. Do you know that dog never offered to cross that highway again?

My mailbox is on the other side of it. Kaedo would always follow me to the end of the drive, sit down and wait for me to come back over, pet him on the head and tell him what a good boy he was.

No matter where I was working on the property he was either right beside me or constantly looking over to see if I was okay He was the best friend I ever had.

Then, when the situation changed here and God knew I'd no longer be able to take care of him properly I believe he took him home. I found a knot behind his ear and within a week his body was completely covered in them. It was a common cancer for golden retrievers. I had to have him put to sleep. He would've been eight years old the following January 1.

I was sitting at the dining room table on that day, looking out the window and thinking of Kaedo. One of the hooks I have under the maple tree has a metal bird on top of it. When I first shoved it in the ground Kaedo was just a curious adolescent. I watched him one day as he first discovered that bird, thinking it was real. He stopped, crouched, crawled a couple feet, strained to see then proceeded to make the same movements several times before he finally worked his way up to the tree.

It was the funniest thing to see his reaction when he finally realized the bird wasn't real. He'd thought he was a great bird hunter!

As I was smiling and pondering that day a big yellow dog sauntered into view. It went out to the tree, sniffed the bird feeders and walked off toward the back yard. I jumped up from the table and ran to open the back door. Although I whistled, it paid no attention as it slowly made its way through the back yard and disappeared over the little hill.

I'd never seen that dog before or since that January 1 after Kaedo passed, the day that should've been his birthday. Maybe, just maybe he was letting me know he's waiting over the "rainbow bridge" in heaven.

JUST THIS SIDE OF HEAVEN IS
A PLACE CALLED RAINBOW BRIDGE.

When an animal dies that has been especially close to someone here, that pet goes to Rainbow Bridge. There are meadows and hills for all of our special friends so they can run and play together. There is plenty of food and water and sunshine, and our friends are warm and comfortable. All the animals who had been ill and old are restored to health and vigor; those who were hurt or maimed are made whole and strong again, just as we remembered them in our dreams of days and times gone by.

The animals are happy and content, except for one small thing; they miss someone very special to them, who had to be left behind.

They all run and play together, but the day comes when one suddenly stops and looks into the distance. The bright eyes are intent; the eager body quivers. Suddenly he begins to break away from the group, flying over the green grass, his legs carrying him faster and faster. YOU have been spotted, and when you and your special friend finally meet, you cling together in joyous reunion, never to be parted again. The happy kisses rain upon your face; your hands again caress the beloved head, and you look once more into the trusting eyes of your pet, so long gone from your life but never absent from your heart.

Then you cross Rainbow Bridge together.

Anonymous

The WOG

In June of 2004 I found out Danny was doing something that finished off my heart. From that day on I merely existed. My prayers intensified to the point that I was begging God for some relief. I couldn't remember praying that desperately since my childhood when my father was beating and molesting me the first thirteen years of my life. It would be over four more long years before my husband of three decades would finally fall in love with a younger woman, ask her to marry him and file for a divorce from me - in that order. It was divine intervention.

By April of 2007 the pain in my right shoulder had become almost unbearable. I finally sought a neurosurgeon and made an appointment. He promptly scheduled an MRI. The results showed a torn rotator cuff with arthritic changes and fluid build up. There is a complete tear of the infraspinatus tendon and a partial tear of the supraspinatus tendon.

In layman terms the rotator cuff consists of four tendons, one on the top, one on the bottom and one on each side. They were described to me as "rubber bands." My rear one is completely torn and the one on top is partially torn. It takes tremendous force to tear a healthy rotator cuff.

Discussing the options with me, the doctor suggested surgery but emphasized that there were no guarantees he could repair it. The other option was therapeutic exercises and a shot of cortisone. I opted for the second choice, received the shot along with a short lesson on the therapy and was sent home with some exercise bands.

Some of the movements require looping the elastic band around a door knob, closing the door and stretching the band with my right arm. Since Troy's room was unoccupied it seemed like the logical place to conduct my routine.

One particular day I was washing the bedding in his old room and had the mattress and box spring off so I could wash the dust ruffle which covered a piece of plywood on the bottom. I was standing in there doing the therapy pondering my situation, talking to God. I was afraid I was making the wrong choices, that maybe I should pack up and leave. I'd made so many past mistakes that I was afraid to do anything for fear it would be wrong. Still, I just didn't know how much longer I could go on in the present situation. My anxiety attacks were worsening and I was terrified my heart was going to give out and I wouldn't be there for Terra and the grandchildren. I was deep in discussion with God over all this when I looked down at the plywood on Troy's bed and saw the letters, "W O G."

Immediately I thought, "WOG - Wait on God." How in the world did that get there? Did Troy write them? We'd had this bed set up like this for years, moved from state to state, washed the bedding over and over, yet I'd never, ever before noticed those letters. It was like they just appeared out of nowhere!

I felt immediate peace, God really was listening. The WOG would continue to not only carry me through the next few years but the rest of my life. I know without a doubt it is a special message from God to wait for him to take care of me in his own way, in his own time and he has.

After a few months of doing the therapy I went back to the doctor and he talked me into the surgery. I couldn't shake the uneasy feeling I had as Danny drove me to the hospital that day. I'd previously had surgery to have two discs fused together in my neck and shortly after that I had two disc reductions in my lower back. With both of those surgeries I was anxious and ready, almost happy to get them done. However, this one was different. It just didn't feel right.

My nerves were on edge as I checked in at the desk and my anxiety escalated as they prepped me for the surgery. I bet I made half dozen trips into the bathroom with an I.V. bag trailing along behind me. By the time the news came on at noon I was totally frazzled.

I thought, "Okay God, I just don't feel right about this, what do you want me to do?" Immediately a story came on CNN about a 53 year old lady who had surgery and died three days later from an infection. I asked Danny to go get the nurse, I was going home!

I couldn't believe I had actually walked out of there and not a minute too soon as they were on the way to get me for their last surgery. Looking back I feel I made the right decision. As long as I keep up with the exercises my shoulder doesn't bother me too much, except when I try to sleep on it. I am able to dig dirt, plant flowers, pull weeds and take care of almost twelve acres all alone and that includes mowing over half of it. There is no way I could accomplish these things if I weren't receiving His special graces. I am still listening and trusting Him to take care of me.

Sometime later I had the thought that maybe I'd imagined the WOG so I went in Troy's old room, raised the dust ruffle and scooted the mattress and box spring over. Nope, I hadn't imagined it. I took a picture.

Sitting at my little kitchen table one day I was thinking about the WOG. So I said, "Okay God, now that I've got it what do you want me to do with it? I heard, "write it down." So I did, then I said, "now what?" Then I heard, "license plates, business cards and billboards."

I obtained a trademark and set about fulfilling what I thought was his wish. I bought business cards and I ordered license plates. Janice said the license plate looks mean; so I made it happy. I told her He's not mean, He's mad! Maybe the WOG is meant to be a message from Him to the world. Isn't it obvious every time you listen to the news and weather? There are so many devastating floods, tornadoes, hurricanes, earthquakes and etc.? He's very mad and I believe He's trying to tell us we better wake up and remember who He is before it's too late!

I dreamed of a billboard on every interstate in the good ole USA. I started taking down 800 numbers to call every time I passed one with it posted, even had Janice and Audie get some numbers as they drove over on Interstate 70. Then I started calling them. Well, I couldn't afford that! I had zero income and no job prospects. Now what do I do God?

A cross I'd seen outside Effingham, Illinois came to mind. I researched it on the internet and discovered it was called, "The Cross Foundation." There is a 198' cross at the intersection of I-70 and I-57 that is a beacon of hope to the projected 50,000 travelers that pass it each day. Beneath it are the Ten Commandments. I remember the first time I saw it. It was so awesome! The wonderful feeling never fades. Every time I see it I'm totally humbled.

I thought perhaps if I wrote them and explained my dilemma they might have enough spare room on their property to put up a billboard if I paid for it. I figured I could spare the initial cost if I didn't have to pay a monthly rental fee.

How wonderful they've been. I received a letter back saying that although they didn't have the space at the cross there was a man with an empty bulletin board west of Vandalia, Illinois who was willing to donate the rental fee to me for three months if I'd pay the $400 for the vinyl.

I'd done it! Well, at least there was ONE bulletin board going up and considering how it all happened I was even more convinced that God was working on this project. I opened a web site to sell the license plates and offered to donate $5 of every sale to the church or charity of the purchaser. Unfortunately, www.wogwaitongod.com didn't produce much. So I've lowered the price of the plates and deleted the $5 offer.

I find myself wondering if perhaps the WOG experience was actually just supposed to be another chapter in this book. A chapter God wants written.

Orbs

After contemplating the orbs and researching them on the computer I've come to the conclusion that there may be several different varieties. Everything from dust particles, bursts of energy, ghosts, good spirits and angels.

I believe my orb is Troy, an angel. I've had the same camera for years; however, the orb didn't show up until after he passed. Not only that, it only shows up on special occasions and in special spots. In our four generations picture it was right above my head and he has never, not once, shown up in a picture that Danny was in.

Terra's twenty-third birthday rolled around, the first one without Troy here to celebrate and she and I were standing in the kitchen talking. All of a sudden she stopped, got an amazing look on her face and said, "I just saw Troy!" I said, "Huh?" She said, "I just saw Troy walk down the hallway headed to his room!" Needless to say she was ecstatic and I wasn't the least bit surprised as he'd made his presence so well known the past five months. Terra was elated that he'd shown up for her birthday and the very next year it happened again. Only this time she just caught a glimpse of his blue jeaned leg as it was passing the hallway door. Still, she was happy and certain that he'd made an appearance on her special day.

By the time April 5th rolled around the following year she was dating her soon to be husband so he was here for our little celebration. I baked her favorite cake, a yellow butter recipe with homemade fudge icing. It was adorned with twenty five candles glowing bright on the top. She was finally moving on and smiling again. Terra grinned like her old self after accomplishing the task of blowing out all those candles with one breathe then anxiously opened her gifts.

Suddenly, I noticed a sad expression. What's wrong I asked? "Troy didn't show up for my birthday this year," she said. I assured her the day wasn't over and asked her to stand up for a picture with Jeff and DanTerrah.

I was anxious to show her the downloaded pictures. It seems Troy was there all along.

I found myself wondering how he could show up in different forms and my thoughts started to reach deeper into the mysteries of life and what comes after our passing. I began to read books about angels and heaven, spirits and anything else I thought might give me some insight into life after death. The more I read the more mysterious it became. The only thing I knew for absolute certainty, Troy was still able to be here for us.

Soon Terra was expecting her son Tobin and we were at her in-laws for a baby shower. Terra was in her element.

All the attention was placed on her and the son she was carrying. Her mother in law, Rita, and Rita's sisters had done a wonderful job for the occasion and all I had to do was sit back, take a few pictures and enjoy the moment. It was fun.

This time I was the one surprised when the pictures were downloaded.

The first time I saw the orb on Terra's stomach I thought perhaps Troy's spirit had entered her unborn child but just as quickly I realized that couldn't be true. He's still giving obvious signs of his presence with us.

So what could the orb on her belly be? This one still raises a lot of questions in my mind and might make a great argument for the anti abortionist group. One thing I've come to realize, angels or spirits definitely enjoy celebrations.

Jaidan sure didn't like that fancy hat her Nanny had bought for her second birthday.

Mom said, "Hurry, take a picture before she jerks it off!" It looks like her ever protecting father was watching the scene from just a foot or two above her head.

My mother was heart broken when Troy passed. He was her first born grandchild and she still can hardly talk about him without tearing up. Just a couple weeks ago she was telling me she'd kept the living room end table that he'd cut his teeth on for years and now that he's passed she regrets ever letting it go. She loved his big smile and he was always saying, "I love you nanny" and giving her little gifts and big hugs. Christmas of 2007 I was up at her house in Minnesota and she and I took a picture together. When it was downloaded we saw a big orb right next to moms' heart. Now she knows for sure he's still with her.

Me and Mom

2007 Mom and Troy's last picture together

Special Gifts

Just a couple mornings ago I was standing at my kitchen window watching a squirrel eating the seeds dropped from the maple tree. All of a sudden a little chipmunk came running down the stones, leaped on the squirrel then back onto the stone again and was gone in a flash. The stunned squirrel momentarily looked up to see what the heck had happened then went back to his seeds. I had a great laugh and a wonderful start to my morning.

Yesterday I checked out the four blue eggs in my bluebird nest box hanging on the outside of the building where I keep my mowers and tools. My whistle was met with four little beaks sticking up in the air hoping for a tasty bite. Today, watching from inside the house, I got a warm feeling when I saw mom or dad perched on the hole, reaching in to feed them.

Just before I sat down to write this chapter I looked out front and saw two quails waddling across the front lawn. I only get to see those two or three times during the year and always get tickled at how they waddle like a duck.

I feel so blessed to have these special gifts in my life. These God given gifts that we only have to stop, look and listen for are all around us. They are the best. Then there are the gifts from our family and friends.

Mom and Kimble presented me with a beautiful statue of Mary holding the baby Jesus a few Christmases ago. I sat her on a little shelf beside my bed facing forward and enjoyed the comfortable feeling she seemed to give me every time I climbed in and out of my bed.

One morning I woke up, looked up and saw her looking down at me. Somehow, she had turned almost a quarter of a turn around toward the bed (perhaps with the help of an angel). Calming warmth spread through my body. I decided to leave her in that position and eventually put the feather I'd found at the end of the driveway on the return from our vacation under her edge.

However, it was not the end of the miraculous statue. There is a dove nesting on the base of Mary's dress and doves have always been a favorite of mine. One day I counted thirty sitting in my maple tree out front. I always thought the dove on the statue looked like it needed something else.

"Miracles happen to those who believe!" One day I was sitting at my little kitchen table by the window when a dove landed by the sidewalk. It was walking around and acting strangely. Not looking for food, but looking all the same. I thought, "What is that bird doing?" I didn't have to wonder long. She squatted right down in front of me and laid an egg!

Well, of all the special gifts I'd received this one topped the cake! Then she flew off. I couldn't believe it. Of course, being the bird person that I am, I went right out and gathered up that little pure white egg. It was still warm. I said, "Thank you God."

Maybe I could hatch it! The grandkids highchair was only used once or twice a year on their visits from Minnesota and had a plug in close so I decided it would be the perfect spot for a nest. After laying down a heating pad set on low I gently positioned the egg in the center and added a washcloth on top.

I checked it religiously; however, it never produced a little dove. Then it dawned on me. Obviously my special angel had heard my thoughts and brought the perfect item for the dove nesting at the bottom of my statue. It's never rotted and is still there today.

As if this wasn't enough - not long after that I was out front and saw a baby dove in the grass. Nightfall was not too far away and I didn't see mom or dad anywhere. I walked over and gently picked it up. I softly whistled, "pretty bird" and it looked up at me with soulful eyes. I was in love. I carried the little guy inside, sat in my recliner and held it for the longest time on my chest. It was a special feeling.

Thinking perhaps mom and/or dad would be back I found an old flower pot and filled it half full with pine needles and maple leaves. After hanging it in a tree and nestling the baby dove inside I said a quick prayer that it would be okay and went in the house. The next day it was out in the grass again!

Several days before it was old enough to fly I had the pleasure of gathering it up, bringing it in for a visit and putting it to bed in the tree. Mom and dad fed it regularly.

Mom and Kimble were here for a visit not too long afterwards and we were all in the kitchen when a dove flew into the grass outside close to the house. I'd sent them a picture of me holding the baby so they knew the story.

I said, "I wonder if that could be my dove?" Believing it was a one in a million shot I decided to walk outside and see if it stayed put. A wild dove never would have. I couldn't believe it. I opened the front door, starting whistling "pretty bird" and it just looked at me. I slowly walked over, whistling as I went and crouched down within two or three feet of that dove and it never flew away. I didn't want to ruin the moment by reaching out and having it fly off so I slowly moved back to the door. I knew it was my dove. I said, "Thank you God (and Troy)." What perfect timing.

Gifts are extra special when they show up unexpectedly. My sister Roxanne visited me last summer from Las Cruces, New Mexico. She's the baby so there's eight years between us. I hadn't spent much time around her since we were kids so it was nice to have a special bonding vacation with just the two of us.

One day we decided to go antique shopping. I'd heard of a huge shop in downtown Terre Haute with several booths I'd wanted to check out so off we went. As soon as we walked through the doors we knew it would take a long time to get through and were anxious to see what kind of treasures we might uncover.

I didn't have to wonder long. As soon as we walked into the first booth I spotted it. Was I seeing things? No, I gently lifted it off the shelf and felt my grateful heart singing.

It was a beautiful little Noritake bone china limited edition heart. There was a young man in a field of flowers holding a dove in one hand and a key in the other. At the bottom it said, "Valentine 1973." Troy was born in 1973. Was it a coincidence? There are no coincidences.

Steve Warner
Glen Campbell
The Hand That
Rocks The Cradle

1-800-HOLIDAY

Mom has felt the need to give me gifts on Mothers Day, Christmas and my birthday since Troy's passing which she says are from him, that he led her to them for me. She will be in a store and something will tell her to go to a certain spot. When she gets there she always seems to find just one of a particular item that fits this scenario perfectly. An angel bear, a little boy angel, most recently a little boy figurine holding a bouquet of flowers and a book that says, "I love you mom." These are just a small sampling of the many gifts she's presented me with in the past seven and a half years.

I'm truly blessed to have such a special mom. Most of the gifts she gives me nowadays have an angel theme. One Christmas she brought me a beautiful Lucite angel from Steven Lavaggi; the internationally recognized, "Artist of Hope." This particular angel led to a series of events that in the end presented me with one of my most treasured possessions. A true miracle delivery!

Terra had admired the Lucite angel so I decided to order one for her. I waited, and waited, and waited yet nothing arrived so I emailed the company. The artist's wife, Audrey, emailed me right back, apologized and assured me the box would be sent right out.

It arrived in a timely manner and I anxiously opened it. What! This isn't what I ordered. I ordered the white angel, this one's black. I wanted the white one like I had for Terra. I emailed her back and she could not have been more gracious and apologetic. She immediately responded that after my last email her husband had gone out to the factory and let the workers have it for not getting the first box sent and now they'd sent the wrong item. She felt so bad that I felt bad for having to complain. What a nice lady she is.

Instructing me to keep the black angel or give it away she assured me her husband would go out in the factory himself, pack up my angel and send it to me by special delivery. I anxiously waited.

That afternoon I had an appointment with my beautician to get my hair trimmed and was stunned to hear her tell me she had just buried her mother a few days prior. I hadn't heard. She started telling me that her mother absolutely loved Halloween and her all time favorite thing was to dress up as a witch and greet the kids at the door as the wicked witch. She had said that when she dies she wants them to sing, "The wicked witch is gone, the wicked witch is gone! " Unfortunately that seemed to present Karen with a problem. Now every time she thought of her mom all she could picture in her head was a black wicked witch flying around in the sky. Oh, poor Karen.

I'd no sooner pulled my vehicle out of her driveway when it hit me like a ton of bricks! So that's why I received the black angel instead of the white one! I went home, grabbed the black angel and headed right back over to Karen's. I presented her with the angel and told her now she could picture her mom as an angel flying around instead of a witch. She was thrilled with the gift and there is a beautiful Lucite black angel displayed high on a shelf in her shop. No, there are no coincidences.

The next day my "white" angel arrived FedEx but the artist and his wife had gone way above and beyond making up for the mistake of their employees. The more I dug the more I found! A red, white and blue angel pin, angel decals, and an angel bracelet which was perfect for Terra. It had five little angels on it. There were three female colors and two male colors and it was perfect for her family of three girls and two boys. Terra loved it.

Then I saw it. Tears came to my eyes. It was a beautiful sterling silver bracelet engraved with an angel and my favorite psalm, 91:11. "He will give His Angels charge over you, to keep you in all your ways."

I can't even begin to express in this book the comfort this bracelet has given me for only a real angel could've known exactly what I and his sister needed. It was another confirmation that God had allowed my special angel to be here on earth watching over us. Mr. and Mrs. Lavaggi will always have my eternal gratitude for their extreme generosity. They are so special.

I took the bracelet to my jeweler and had him engrave Troy's name, birth date, and November 6, 2002 on the back.

My Thoughts and Wishes

It's often said, "Be careful what you wish for, you might just get it." Seems that's exactly what's been happening to me the past few years. I have moved from just thinking it is possible to knowing it is. It's as if someone is enjoying fulfilling my very thoughts and wishes.

Just like the two purses I found when I walked into a popular discount store yesterday. I'd previously looked at them on the internet but decided I really didn't "need" them. Well, who could walk away when they were less than half the price!

Or take the time I was planning to get my garden ready for planting. I don't need a lot of vegetables these days so I've taken to putting in more flowers than food. Also, I've found that if I put black plastic down, poke holes in it for seeds and plants I don't have to worry about hoeing weeds. So, contemplating the next day's project one night I was wondering if I had enough plastic left over from last year out in the building to finish the job. Certainly can't imagine why I worried over the small stuff now.

Up early so I could get finished with the garden before the sweltering heat set in, I finished my breakfast and prayers; grabbed my gloves and headed out the door. Thinking I probably should've checked the plastic before the last minute I glanced in the direction of the highway and something caught my eye.

What is that out there? No, it couldn't be. My steps became quicker as I got closer. Well, I'll be darned, I can't believe it. It's plastic! Black plastic!

Not only was there one long piece on my side of the highway, there was another one on the other side. Brand new too. Now that's the kind of trash I like gathering up. What perfect timing. Guess my angel has been listening again. I was so excited I took a picture of it with my cell phone and called mom to tell her a picture was on the way to their email of my latest miracle.

Lying in bed one night I was unable to fall asleep. Praying hard I was worrying about a situation I had no control over. All of a sudden a musical doll sitting over in the corner of the bedroom started playing music. It felt like a message from beyond telling me I wasn't alone; everything would be okay and sleep quickly followed.

Shopping for clothes has become a breeze. I needed a special outfit for Terra's wedding and had decided exactly what it would look like. The next day I walked into the store, over to the first rack of clothes and found the exact outfit I'd imagined; in my size and on sale. It happens all the time.

When Troy passed, my cousin Sherri sent me a subscription to *The Marian Helper*, a catholic magazine. The September 2006 issue arrived with a picture of Jesus on it and an article about the Divine Mercy.

On February 22, 1931, Jesus appeared to Sister Faustina Kowalski who was a sister of Our Lady of Mercy. He instructed her to paint a picture of the image she saw with the signature: Jesus I Trust In You. He wanted the image venerated and honored throughout the world.

Eventually, she was able to fulfill his wishes. Many people have received amazing graces by venerating or honoring the photo. I felt drawn to the image, ordered a copy then prayed for the perfect frame before I headed off to Wal-Mart and it was there waiting. It was just perfect, not taking away from the photo but adding to it.

The last part of April has become a special time of year for me here in southern Indiana. Not only do my hummingbirds find their way back home; the big morel mushrooms start showing up in the woods. You haven't lived until you've had a wild morel rolled in flour, fried in a big skillet full of butter and sprinkled with salt and pepper. They're a real delicacy, however, that first bite still comes in second to the thrill of hunting for them.

Since Danny was manager of the local coal mine we had our pick of some of the best spots available. We enjoyed tromping through the woods for years every spring and always had a bet as to who would find the first one. Nine times out of ten he would spot it. Funny thing about morels; seems that first one of the season is really hard to pin down but once you catch sight of that wonderful mushroom it's as if your eyes are retrained into spotting them the rest of the season, which is way too short.

This area is great if you like to explore the woods. We have very few snakes and none that are poisonous. In fact, in all the years we hunted I can only remember seeing three snakes. Heck, I've had more than that in my own yard. I think they took up residence here when the house sat empty for a few years. It took years to get rid of the majority of them.

Danny and I headed off for our usual mushroom hunting route. I couldn't quite put my finger on it but something just didn't feel right. I felt uneasy, maybe a little scared. I'd become untrusting of him and found myself wishing I hadn't come along that day. Normally, he would hold the tree limbs back for me as we walked our familiar path but on this particular hunt he was more apt to let them slap me in the face. The deeper into the woods we ventured the more uneasy I felt.

About half way up to our favorite spot he stopped dead in his tracks. He'd almost stepped on a huge black snake that was stretched across a fallen tree. I thought, "That was strange, we've never even seen a snake in this area." It felt like a bad omen. By the time we arrived at the destination I was a basket case inside and couldn't even think about finding a mushroom.

All of a sudden a very tall, very well built good looking man came out of the woods headed in our direction carrying a plastic sack. I remember thinking, why is he coming from that direction; the woods are too thick to get through. He sauntered up, gave a big smile and asked how the mushroom hunting was going. Danny shot back, "this is mine property, and you're not supposed to be in here if you don't have a permit." I felt like crawling under a rock. The guy just said "okay" and kept walking.

As he passed us I looked down at the full plastic bag he was carrying and that's when I noticed them. He didn't have any mushrooms in that bag; there was just a bunch of old weeds sticking out the end of it. Then it dawned on me, he had to be an angel. At that moment I knew I was being watched over and didn't have to worry anymore.

Feeling like a ton of bricks had been lifted off my shoulders I thought to myself, "now let me find the biggest mushroom of all." At that very instant I looked down in front of my feet and saw a whopper of a mushroom! The biggest one I'd ever found before or since. I said, "Thank you God for my special guardian angel."

Several years ago I had spotted the perfect dogwood tree for the center of our driveway; it was about fifteen feet tall with plenty of branches. We took our shovels in, dug it up and hauled it home.

Although we already had a couple at the edge of the woods on the west side of the house that bloomed faithfully each spring, the one in the driveway was extra special and I babied and watched over it like a mother hen that first year making sure it had plenty of water. It flourished. All three of the trees were white.

A few years later I noticed it was not looking too well and my residential woodpecker was constantly pecking away at it. Discussing this problem with my friend Becky one day she suggested spraying it with an insecticide. Not completely comfortable with that I logged onto an internet chat room and presented the problem.

Someone was kind enough to answer back that the woodpecker was eating the worms that were killing the tree and if I would just ignore it and let nature take its course the tree should be fine.

I don't know who I was more thankful for, the internet friend or the woodpecker who saved my precious dogwood tree. Every spring it's full of beautiful white flowers.

This past year on a trip to Georgia I found myself admiring the many pink dogwood trees they have in Savannah and wishing I had one. Did I say I was "wishing" I had a pink dogwood tree?

As usual, spring arrived and all three were full of beautiful white blossoms. At least until I pulled in the driveway from church one Sunday. Admiring my dogwood tree in the center before pulling in the garage caused me to put the vehicle in park and get out. I couldn't believe it, my white dogwood tree was pink! How beautiful.

My mind was racing and I quickly walked over to the edge of the woods and checked the other two trees. They were both still white! I had to compare to make sure I wasn't seeing things so I pulled some petals off each tree and took them over to the house. The driveway tree was definitely pink. I can't count the trips I made to that tree this spring before the blossoms all dropped off. It was just perfect. I felt so blessed.

THE LEGEND OF THE DOGWOOD TREE

In Jesus' time, the dogwood grew
To a stately size and a lovely hue.

'Twas strong and firm, its branches interwoven
For the cross of Christ its timbers were chosen.

Seeing the distress at this use of their wood
Christ made a promise which still holds good.

'Never again shall the dogwood grow
Large enough to be used so.

Slender and twisted, it shall be
With blossoms like the cross for all to see.

As blood stains the petals marked in brown
The blossom's center wears a thorny crown.

All who see it will remember Me
Crucified on a cross from the dogwood tree.

Cherished and protected this tree shall be
A reminder to all of My agony.

Last year the Japanese beetles were just horrendous. I'd long ago given up trying to spray for them because I don't want to harm the birds and animals I have in the area. One of my gardening books said to pick them off by hand and drop them in a pail of soapy water. As cruel as it sounded I decided to give it try. Worked like a charm but I found myself feeling bad about drowning them and wishing there was a better way.

The next day I noticed something strange on the concrete behind my "pot man" which I had sitting on a large plastic spool in the corner of the patio. Further investigation caused my jaw to drop. There in a form similar to the shape of angels wings were a bunch of dead beetles! HA - ask and ye shall receive. Or in my case seems I just need to think about it. There was nothing back there that should've killed those beetles; it had never happened before.

dead beetle bugs

Speaking of that patio I had never liked the color of it since we had it poured as it seemed to me that ugly gray stuck out like a sore thumb against the stonework on this house. I sure was wishing we had put some kind of color in the concrete before it was poured.

The color of the patio wasn't the only thing that was bugging me around that time. Our shingles on the roof really needed replacing. Every time there was a storm Danny had to crawl up and replace a few. We get plenty of wind and rain in the spring and fall of the year. Spring blows in and fall blows out - both with a vengeance.

We had a doozy come through one night. So many shingles were off that we decided maybe we'd call our insurance company even though we almost knew they wouldn't do anything. Luck, something or someone was on our side. A tornado had gone through and done a lot of damage two towns over. In fact my neighbor Gert has a brother living there who was sitting in his living room watching TV when the tornado took everything in the room but the chair he was sitting in and a curio cabinet. Apparently, he has a special angel also.

We were completely surprised when the insurance adjuster told us they would replace all the shingles on our home. The two outbuildings would be excluded. To say we were shocked and thrilled would be an understatement. We just really couldn't believe we'd been so fortunate.

A couple of months later the roofers showed up. Danny and I were out back building a foundation for the swing set so we were able to observe and interact with them. They were very efficient and soon had the job moving along like an assembly line. It was entertaining to watch.

We needed something for our latest outside project so we took the truck down to Lowe's in Vincennes to pick it up. As we pulled back into our driveway we noticed the workers on the roof above the front patio. Then we saw something on the patio. Oh, oh. It was a generator and unbeknown to the guys on the roof it was vibrating itself in circles, taking pieces of our concrete as it rotated.

By the time they were able to stop it we had a fancy etching that resembled a duck. I don't know who felt worse; the roofers that it happened or us for them that it happened. In any case we couldn't live with the quack quack. I could just see Troy smiling up above.

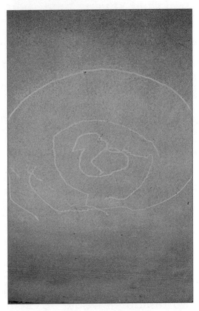

concrete duck

The roofers felt so bad that they shingled both our out buildings with the extra shingles they had left over and the roofing company sent someone to look at our patio.

Of course it was much cheaper to resurface the thing than it would have been to tear it all out and completely replace the whole patio and sidewalk since they would never have been able to match the color if they tried to do just the duck section.

I was beside myself when the man came over with all his color charts. Did I say "color charts?" Yes I did. Looks like we not only had brand new shingles on "both" the house and outbuildings, we also were getting a new top for the patio and it didn't cost us one red cent. I said, "Thank you Troy boy and God." Miracles happen to those who believe!

It seems I have evolved into someone who is actually living what I have believed all my life. That God and his angels are close and here to help us along in this wonderful world. We need only to believe and trust completely to experience a deeper, inner peace and to be an active participant in our universe. As the Dalai Lama says, "A change of heart is always a change of mind. " I believe, "A change of heart and mind is a change of life."

The Rainbow Dress

Danny was working down in South America and I was driving to Evansville to pick Jaidan up. It had been a while since she had been up and I was anxious to see her. She was into rainbows and Hanna Montana these days. When I asked her what she wanted the recently remodeled grandkids' room decorated in she said rainbows, so I painted one wall red, the other three white and put all the different colors of the rainbow in it. The first thing she said was, "why didn't you paint a yellow and green and purple wall?"

She was seven years old now and looking more like her daddy every time I saw her. It amazes me how many of his mannerisms she has considering he hasn't been here to pass them on. She even chews her tongue like he always did. She's definitely her daddy's daughter and it warms my heart to see that so many of his looks and moves are still here.

She headed right into the house ready to play as soon as we pulled in the garage. Her energy keeps us both on the move while she's here and I find myself realizing it's a good thing we have children in our younger years. However, I seem to keep up with the various activities we get into. Playing Barbie, pitching a ball back and forth, putting puzzles together, squirt guns in the hot tub, coloring and drawing pictures, putting make-up on her dolls and painting her fingernails and theirs are just a few of the things we enjoy sharing. Her favorite activity is sitting down on an old board and wrapping her legs around a rope tied to the pine tree out back while I swing her around within inches of the tree base. Grandkids are special.

The next day we decided to run up to Terre Haute, grab an Arby's and stop by the childrens' second-hand store to see what kind of treasures we could come up with. With four grandchildren between the ages of two and seven I enjoy dropping in there from time to time. They quickly grow out of clothes at these ages so it's great we have a place where we can recycle their gently used items.

It was a cloudy day with just a few blue areas shining through. About three miles down the highway something caught my eye so I pulled over to the side and asked Jaidan what that cloud looked like. Without hesitating she said, "Jesus." That was exactly what I had been thinking. The perfect profile looked as if it was peering through the edge of the blue area at us. I was quick to grab my phone and take a picture before we continued down the highway.

It wasn't until we were home again that I decided to look at the picture. Woops, guess I was too quick taking that picture since it was my face staring back. Darn, I'd obviously taken it in the wrong direction. How disappointing.

The store is packed with clothes at this time of year (after most have bought their summer things but before they've started school shopping) it's a struggle to separate them enough to see what you want to see.

Jaidan followed me for awhile then became bored and asked if she could play with the children in the little play area they have set up in the corner of the room. I gave her the go ahead and finished getting a few size twos for Karsynn and threes for Tobin before I went over to the area where she was playing. DanTerrah's sevens and Jaidan's eights were in that aisle.

I found a few nice things for DanTerrah but Jaidan's were really picked over. By the time they get to that size they are more apt to be worn out and the pickings get fewer and farther between. Three times I went through that rack and was only able to find a couple of nice things. Oh, well. Maybe I'd have better luck the next time.

I practically had to pry her away from the play area. We were walking past the rack I'd just dissected with a fine tooth comb when Jaidan said, "Look Mamatae, a rainbow dress. Can I have it?" You could've knocked me over with a feather. Sure enough, sticking out in plain sight was a pretty little dress just perfect for the little girl that loves rainbows.

I'd been through that rack three times, I would have seen it. Apparently I'm not the only one receiving special gifts. I told Jaidan I'd looked and looked through that rack of clothes and didn't see that dress so her daddy must've put it there just for her to find. Jaidan was a "happy girl."

Standing in my living room a few days after she had gone home, I saw that profile again. This time I grabbed my digital camera, however, by the time I made it back to snap the picture it had started dissipating. I took one anyway and sent it on to mom telling her the story of the two profiles.

She called to point out what I had missed. On the backside of the profile of Jesus that I hadn't been able to capture was a perfect profile of a little girl that looked just like me as a child. How interesting. I've received so many special blessings since Troy's passing.

Scents and Movements

Ever so often I'll get a slight scent of Troy's old cologne in the air, most often when I'm driving somewhere thinking about him. It's as if he wants to give me a little reminder that he's still riding with me. Doesn't surprise me considering all the trips we made together, just the two of us.

The day I started this book I walked into his old bedroom and looked around, remembering all the things that had happened since he last slept in my great grandmothers old iron bed. She had specifically specified that I was the one to get it when she passed and I've treasured it ever since.

I spent many days and nights with her as a child. I'm sure she used to bounce me on her knees when I was a toddler. I'd watch her with the little ones tottering on the edge of her knees as she held their hands, bounced them up and down and sang, "trot little horsy, trot to town; don't fall down." Then she would part her knees and they would drop almost to the floor before she stopped their fall; eyes would get big as saucers. She thought it was so funny! I've enjoyed continuing the tradition with my grandbabies. When night fell I was always allowed the honor of crawling in beside her on top of a big, fluffy feather mattress that covered the top. I felt safe. We'd say our prayers then our last words would be - goodnight.

I'll never forget one particular night. Apparently, grandmother had gotten hard of hearing. We said our prayers but before I had a chance to say goodnight I accidentally passed some really loud gas! Grandmother answered, "Goodnight." To this day I can't help smiling to myself every time I think of it and I **never** told her about it.

This is what was going through my head when I was standing in Troy's old bedroom and I caught a light scent of his cologne in the air. Can't remember if I ever told him that story but I'm sure he knows it now.

He had a gun cabinet we'd given him several years ago. I didn't want to keep any guns in it but at the same time I didn't want to get rid of it. The idea entered my mind to put his high school letterman's jacket on display with some of his trophies and ribbons. It worked out very well.

There was plenty of room for his baseball and bowling trophies and of course his special high jump ribbons. I hammered little nails along the notched shelf where the guns used to nestle and hung his ribbons on them; added some pictures and a certificate along with his graduation tassels. Even had a spot up on the shelf to put the little stuffed graduation guy I gave him at his graduation that said, "Way to go" on the pendant he was holding. The cabinet hasn't been opened since we put it on the landing above the living room. I look in it regularly as I often open the coat closet it's standing by.

One day I noticed things had moved. It was shortly after my divorce was finalized. Troy had tried to convince me to go through with the divorce in 1998 so I knew he wanted me out of the situation. Apparently he was sending me a clear message that he was happy I was free.

Down in the far left bottom corner of the gun cabinet lies the little graduation guy that says, "Way to go" along with one of his high jump medals. The medal had been securely nailed to the shelf on the far right side of the cabinet. It was a clear sign - Troy approved of the divorce.

It may have been possible for that doll to fall off the shelf above but very unlikely it could've landed into that perfect position. Still, there is no way that medal could've gotten from the position it was in to the spot where it now rests.

My sister Janice was up visiting from South Carolina. We share a lot of the same beliefs so I wanted to show her the gun cabinet. She calls me, "Sisser."

After explaining it to her she gives me a most serious look and says, "Now, sisser - you and I know God and he does amazing things but he did not do this." No, probably not, but angels obviously do.

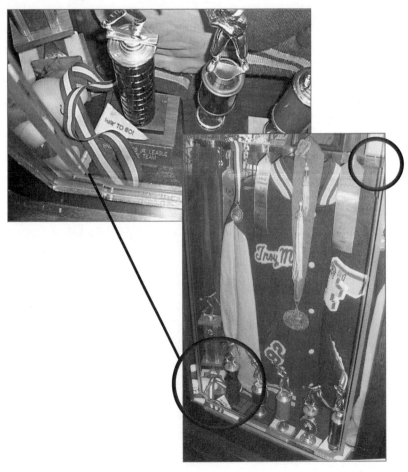

Yes, most of us know that God's angels have been given the power to do monumental feats. I just never realized they would actually do small things to let us know we are never alone. My whole concept of what goes on around us has changed since Troy passed.

Remember the day DanTerrah and I was sitting at the dining room table when she stopped to listen to the man above the flower arrangement, the man who went out the window? That wasn't the end of the episode. We had put the letters to the alphabet in their proper slots and I'd placed them high above a cabinet in the kitchen.

The next morning when I climbed out of bed and walked past the dining room to the kitchen I noticed something yellow on the floor next to my Mamareney's sewing machine.

She had sewed so many clothes for me when I was a child, before she had the stroke. It paralyzed her for eleven years and she was bedridden up until her passing. I was blessed when I inherited her love of sewing and other crafts.

When I was old enough I used her sewing machine to mend Granddaddy's pants so he wanted me to have it when he passed. Not only does the old Singer still work, it has outlasted the one Danny bought for me before we were married. Mamareney's machine is the one I depended on to finish Karsynn's baby quilt after mine crashed. I love that old sewing machine and the fond memories I have of her sitting at it making me something special.

I looked down; there, leaning up against one leg was a yellow M! How had it gotten from the top of the kitchen cabinet to that floor? Also, did Mamareney do it or Troy? His last name is Mills.

My Daughter's Story

Even though there was six years difference between Troy and Terra they were always close. That's not to say they never had a fight, there was plenty of those around the house while they were growing up but when it came to taking care of each other they were pretty tight. So, not surprisingly, the day she decided to put the crib together for the child she was carrying he was the one sitting on the floor helping her out.

kids with buffalo in the background, and at graduation

Troy and Terra mounting crib

Terra was naturally devastated when she couldn't sit and chat with him anymore. However, DanTerrah was born the following March so she found herself concentrating on the daughter who looked so much like her brother Troy.

When DanTerrah was about a year and a half old Terra had a strong yearning to visit her brother Darryl in Arizona. It was as if she had to find out if he was still there so we put her and DanTerrah on a plane so they could visit Darryl and his family for a week.

Unfortunately, DanTerrah became very ill almost as soon as they arrived. Almost the entire week was spent running back and forth to the pharmacy and cleaning up vomit. The day before they were to leave she was finally able to keep her food down so Darryl took them and his two children, Justus and Skylar, to visit the Grand Canyon.

The next day it was time for the long drive from Flagstaff to Phoenix where they would board a plane to come home. Terra was functioning on very little sleep, worrying and praying DanTerrah wouldn't get sick on the plane and they would make it home okay.

Her anxiety disappeared when she looked down and saw a single white feather resting on her jeans. She knew that both of her brothers were still there for her and that she and DanTerrah would be just fine. She took a picture and they had a pleasant flight home.

Terra-Darryl-Troy, 1989

Terra decided to attend Indiana Business College in Terre Haute where she met Jeff. He was in Terre Haute attending Indiana State University to get his Masters in Geology and they found each other on an internet dating site. After graduation she took a position at a clinic and they continued seeing each other. Jeff graduated and was offered a job in northern Minnesota not far from the Canadian border.

Before they moved north we all flew to Las Vegas for a whirlwind wedding at the Aladdin hotel and casino. Considering how quick everything was thrown together it turned out to be a beautiful ceremony and a memorable trip. Too soon they were packing up to go north.

We talked several times on the phone each day and it wasn't long before Terra and DanTerrah were flying home for a visit and the baby shower at her mother-in-law's. Danny and I picked them up in Indianapolis.

DanTerrah had grown so fast and Terra's belly was also growing. She had a special glow. Married life and Minnesota seemed to agree with her. It was good to see them again. We stopped at the Steak and Shake before embarking on the one and a half hour drive home.

Everyone was relieved when we pulled into the garage and we were all ready to get out of the vehicle and stretch our legs. As soon as we entered the hallway through the back door the paper shredder started up, and then turned itself back off after a few seconds! The same paper shredder we'd had for years. Never before had it started up on its own and it never did again after that day. I looked at Terra and said, "Well, I guess Troy's glad to see you guys!" What a nice surprise welcome home for them.

The visit was over way too soon and they were gone again. They were soon settled into their new home, then Tobin showed up on November third. We all noticed how close it was to Troy's birthday of November thirtieth. Tobin just reversed the numbers in his day! Karsynn showed up eleven months later. We refer to them as the "babies" since they're so close together. It's almost like having twins in the family.

Everyday phone calls and visits two or three times a year keep us in touch. The kids always seem to grow so much in between those visits. One morning Terra called me all excited.

She had given the babies a bath the night before and as usual they had played with their plastic alphabets that stick to the wall and some other bath toys. When she woke up and went into the bathroom she couldn't believe her eyes. There, on the wall above the tub were some letters. They were, "HI MN." Hi Minnesota. It seems Troy wanted her to know that no matter where she goes he is still with her. He's still her traveling buddy.

Mother's Day

Being blessed with two very special children has afforded me many wonderful Mothers Days throughout the years. However, I can't say they're always so easy anymore. But that's not to say they're always hard either - just different.

The first few years after Troy passed I had a difficult time making it through a church mass without getting a few tears in my eyes. I miss him, but at the same time I'm glad he's in such a special place where he doesn't have to suffer.

Just the past two or three years I've been thinking about why I haven't received many special signs on Mothers Day. Sometimes I do but most of the time I don't and given all the things that have happened since he passed it's one of those things that always puzzles me.

I was pondering that question when I pulled into the church parking lot this year on Mothers Day. Shoot! I must not have been thinking too clearly that morning. The church and dining room is always packed on that day. I'd probably have to park a quarter mile away!

Deciding to go on past the church since I might get a little closer on the other side I was totally dumbfounded as I rounded the curve. There, right in front of an entry door was a parking spot! Happy Mothers Day to me! Obviously heaven had been tuned into my thoughts that morning.

Although there had been plenty of cars in front of me looking for a space it was still there when I came upon it. Which makes me question - is it possible there could've looked like a car was parked there until I came along? What a wonderful feeling I had going into the church on that particular morning. Although I always pray for my children, grandchildren and other relatives and friends this is the day my own children are uppermost in my mind and I send up special prayers of thanks for them.

Unfortunately, everyone doesn't have people to pray for them. I never really thought much about that until we moved into this house fourteen years ago. Almost immediately strange things started happening.

We would hear strange noises, a door opening or closing when there was no one there. It wasn't just one or two of us experiencing things but all four of us. I was telling my sister, Janice, about it one day and she said, "Why don't you just call him Harvey?" It stuck. From that point on it was, "oh that's just Harvey."

I remember one night when the two kids were out and it was just Danny and I at home. He was sacked out on the couch heavily engrossed in a football game so I decided to go to bed early. I hadn't been lying down too awful long when I heard Troy come in and holler in the hallway so I got up to see how he was doing.

After looking for him in the usual spots I walked into the living room and asked Danny where Troy was? He said, "He didn't come in." I said, "I heard him holler in the hallway." He just looked at me nonchalantly and said, "Yea, I heard it too." That's how accustomed we had all gotten to - Harvey. I went on back to bed.

Harvey would regularly twist my bedroom doorknob at seven a.m. and wake me up. That would've been fine if I was ready to get up but I was not!

I was reading a magazine one day which had an article in it about ghosts. I immediately thought of - Harvey. The writer was from England and he said they regularly deal with ghosts over there. He added some advice: when you meet up with a ghost you can do one of two things. You can either ignore them or you can pray for them because they are people that have died and are stuck here on earth.

Poor Harvey! As catholics we are taught to pray for poor souls in purgatory. Perhaps the people we think of as ghosts are actually just stuck in purgatory!

Well, I was an old hat at praying for people in purgatory so I decided what the heck, I'd give it a try and pray that Harvey makes it on to heaven. When I went to bed that night I sent up special prayers just for him.

Let me tell you - prayers work! The next morning just before Danny's alarm went off I opened my eyes to see ole Harvey looking right at me! Yes he was. He was standing right next to my bed looking down at me.

He was a small man about five feet eight or ten inches tall. I'd guess he was in his seventy's or eighty's and he was wearing a flannel shirt and bib overalls. We locked eyes and my heart leaped into my throat.

Immediately he slowly floated back through a picture of Saint Therese of the little flower that I have hanging on my bedroom wall and was gone.

It was time for Danny to get up for work so I woke him and told him Harvey had just been standing by the bed looking at me and had floated back through Saint Therese's picture on the wall.

I got up and followed him to the bathroom. I was sick to my stomach and shaking inside. Oh my goodness! I couldn't believe it. There was no way I was going back to sleep.

Only later did I calm down and rationalize what I thought might have happened. After all I did say some prayers for him before I fell asleep and it was a religious picture he floated back through. Maybe I'd actually helped him move on.

We never had another sign or noise from Harvey after that day and I'm convinced that we can help those in purgatory with our prayers.

A wise man by the name of Murray once told me that if a spirit appears to you they have a message for you. I hadn't figured out what Harvey wanted to tell me yet, however, like I told Terra on the phone today - I kind of miss old Harvey - he was entertaining.

"Saint Therese "The Little Flower"

I'd phoned Terra today to let her know I was going to include Harvey in the book and wondered if she remembered something I hadn't. Yep, Harvey was like one of the family. She immediately knew who I was talking about.

Terra said she had to take her friend Angie home in the middle of the night one time. I asked her why? Seems her and Angie were sleeping in the living room when Angie woke Terra up and insisted she take her home immediately. Apparently Harvey was turning the television on and off and Angie couldn't sleep. Terra took her home and poor Angie never did spend another night here.

Then Terra said the thing she remembered the most about Harvey was the dead smell.

Oh, yea, I'd forgotten all about that! How in the world could I have forgotten about that rotten smell? It was always showing up in Troy's room. Either one or more of us would walk in and smell it or it would show up after we were already in there. It was a smell like I've never smelled before or since. I thanked Terra for reminding me.

I'd only gone three or four steps when it dawned on me. I called Terra right back. You may have just solved the mystery! What mystery she asked? I told her that Murray had told me that if a spirit appears to you then they usually have a message for you. The dead smell we all smelled in Troy's room: was it a message that he was soon going to be passing on? Maybe it was; I'll never know for sure. Although I do know one thing for sure, the world that we live in everyday is not at all what most of us think it is.

It made me feel good to think maybe I might have helped Harvey move on and it was another confirmation for me that prayers really do work.

I especially believe the ones Mothers send up for their children are heard. We are the ones closest to them. We are the ones who cratered them in our soft tissue for approximately nine months. We are the ones that rock the cradle, well, most of the time.

Troy and I were driving somewhere when a song came on the radio and he told me every time he heard it he thought of me. That it was his song for me. It was "The Hand That Rocks the Cradle" by Glen Campbell. The lyrics say, "The hand that rocks the cradle rules the world."

Yes, the year 2008 was especially full of miracles. I'd enjoyed mass on that Mothers Day and was feeling pretty good when I turned the ignition key on in my vehicle afterwards.

Immediately the radio started playing "The Hand That Rocks the Cradle"; just as quick my tears started flowing. What a special gift.

After Troy's accident they gave me the billfold he was carrying the night of the wreck. I meticulously touched every single item it contained. I came across a little folded piece of paper that looked like he had carried it in his wallet for years. Slowly, I unfolded the little piece of paper that seemed to be so important to him.

Now it would be especially important to me, for there in his own handwriting was the title of the song that reminded him of me.

Back to the Beginning

It's where I need to start to help explain the ending. Back to that week in Kentucky when I was just nineteen years old and feeling all alone. I needed someone special of my very own to love; someone who would always be with me. I decided I'd be just fine raising a child by myself.

I was raised to believe that if you really wanted something all you had to do was pray for it and if it was God's will you would receive it. So it was only natural for me to pray for someone special to love. I knew He was listening but I never expected He would send me the beautiful full reality of a son – my son. Yet, is he really just my son? I guess all along he ultimately belonged to God and he returned to God.

Terry and I were still seeing each other. The night we went out and parked at the entrance of the old Sunset Movie Drive Inn Troy was conceived and the miracle started. Only later did I think of the problems I would face raising him alone. Terry and I were married a few months before he was born.

Troy was always active and excelled at everything he decided to do. He was a natural at all sports and after clearing the high jump bar at 6'6" in the senior year of high school he had plenty of offers for scholarships.

He settled on an offer from Saint Mary's University in North Dakota. He was enjoying his freshman year when he tore the anterior cruciate ligament in his left knee. He called to tell me he had been playing basketball with some of the guys when he twisted wrong and heard something snap.

After the operation to repair the ligament he finished his freshman year and was enjoying the summer back in Montana when a letter arrived from the University.

I walked into his room to see him sitting on his bed, letter in hand; tears streaming down his face. His full ride scholarship had been cancelled and he would not be going back to college as a high jump track star. We were both devastated.

Thrown off course he decided he wanted to drive up to Alaska where he had a friend he'd met in college. He wanted to spend some time exploring Alaska and working in the Alaskan fish factories.

It was the summer John Travolta and Christian Slater were going to be in Lewistown filming "Broken Arrow" and I had read in the newspaper they were looking for some extras to be in the movie. I thought Troy would make the perfect cowboy. I tried to talk him into sticking around for it but he was ready to roam.

What could I say? He had my adventure. I gave him my blessing and asked him to put on his cowboy hat so I could take one last picture before he started his long drive north in his little Mazda truck with the two buddies he had talked into going with him.

Danny, Terra and I were on vacation when we received a call from Troy. His Alaskan buddy had gone back to school which put Troy and his two buddies out on their own and none of them had been able to secure jobs. His two buddies decided they wanted to go home so their parents had bought them airline tickets back to Montana.

Broke, sleeping in the back of his pick-up and all alone he called me for advice. He really wasn't ready to leave the state he'd found so full of beauty. I told him I'd try to find a place to wire him some cash in the morning, to call me back around noon.

Worried sick, it was once again time for some serious prayers for my Troy boy. I fell into a fitful sleep.

The call came a lot earlier than expected the next morning and I could hear the excitement in his voice as soon as I said hello. He had been standing outside of one of the fish factories talking to some other guys when someone walked out and said, "I need one man." My quick thinker yelled, "I'll take it!" Thus began his new smelly adventure.

I sent up a prayer of thanks and enjoyed the rest of our vacation.

Troy loved Alaska but was ready to come back to the lower forty eight by the time the job ended. He had met a girl who needed a ride to Phoenix and offered to pay his gas if he would take her there so off they went.

Phoenix! It was such a big city. Now I was really worried. There was good reason to be, he was constantly calling with one problem or another but he wasn't ready to come back to Montana. He bought a motorcycle and wiped out going about 80 miles an hour on the freeway. I was convinced my constant prayers were the only thing that kept him alive.

One day he called to tell me he'd been in a café with some friends when one of them got in an argument with some other guy. When they walked outside they were met by the other guy and his friends, one of whom held a gun to Troy's head. Good thing my boy was a fast talker and so friendly. Yes, he sure kept me busy with the prayers while he was in Phoenix and I was never so relieved as I was the day he called to tell me he was headed to Kentucky.

It wasn't long after that until we were headed to Indiana. Troy enjoyed finally being close enough to both families that he could drive back and forth. He found a job installing carpet for awhile that he seemed to enjoy and helped his dad on the farm.

He moved up here for awhile and found a job delivering fuel for the local mines in the area then later went back to laying carpet.

He was in between jobs when Danny gave him a position in the warehouse on third shift handing out parts and cleaning. It was a big mistake. It wasn't long before my husband was using that position to hurt me and break Troy's spirit. Eventually, Troy turned in his resignation and went back to Kentucky.

Drinking and drugs became a part of his life. I received a call from his dad that he was in the Union County Jail. I will never know what all happened to him during those 30 days but I heard from Shayna, who had a cousin in there at the same time that they put Troy in a cell with a big black gay man who used to steal his food and smack him up beside of the head with his food tray. I try not to speculate about what else might have happened to him. Shayna's cousin said Troy quit going outside and would just sit on his bed facing the wall.

When Terry picked him up at the end of the 30 days Troy had lost his speech. They went out to Terry's Sister Vicki's house and she rode up to Evansville with them to meet me. Vicki said when they got to the house Troy just went over and sat down without saying anything. She looked at him and thought, "Oh, my God, what happened to Troy."

He was gone, completely. He knew who I was but he couldn't talk. It was a quiet drive home, I was heart broken. I knew I had to get him some help. The psychiatrist I took him to looked me straight in the eye and said, "The son you knew will never be back." A part of me died with him that day.

She put him on a strong medication and set up weekly visits. At home he would just sit in front of the TV or sleep in his room. He was like a zombie. We pulled into the drive in of our favorite hamburger joint one afternoon and he asked what they had there. I think that's when it finally sunk in my brain just how bad of a shape he was in. He really had no clue what the place he'd enjoyed so many times before served.

I filled out tons of paper work for social security disability for him and the doctor was so helpful with her recommendations. Social security called me one day to ask some questions about Troy. The man on the phone asked the question, "What does he do most of the day?" I said, "He watches TV and lies on the floor in his bedroom playing with his baseball card collection." He said, "Okay, thank you".

Troy wanted to spend time in Kentucky with the girl he'd been seeing before he went to jail so I spent many days meeting her in Evansville to transfer him back and forth so he could have his weekly visits at the mental health center.

My heart would break all over again every time I would pick him up. The son who had always been so quick to give me a great big smile and hug couldn't even make eye contact anymore. I was terrified he was going to get into some trouble in Kentucky and end up in prison like so many of our children do these days when they get mixed up with drugs and alcohol. I couldn't stand the thought of what would happen to my tall, handsome son if he ended up in a place like that.

My prayers took on a new urgency. God, please, if my boy is headed for prison, please, please, please take him back home with you. It was the most difficult prayer of my life.

Troy received two checks before the night of the accident then they started going to Shayna. God's timing never ceases to amaze me. Had I not gotten all that paper work filled out properly for him Shayna wouldn't be getting over a thousand dollars a month for Jaidan. Because of those checks they've been able to survive and Jaidan will always have health insurance. It was another reason to thank God.

Back to the day I went down to Terry's house to go through Troy's things. He was about to tell me about his miraculous experience on November 6, 2002.

We had all been so worried about Terry. He hadn't hardly left Troy's casket at the funeral. He looked so lost. We were afraid he might have a heart attack as his loss was so deep.

Since I'd lived all over the United States he and Troy hadn't been able to spend a lot of time together, however, they had become great golfing buddies the past few years and had gotten very close so naturally Troy's death devastated Terry.

On the eve of the eleventh day after the accident he was in his living room watching a movie with his wife when he had the strongest need to walk outside. He got up and without saying a word walked out the back door. The first thing he noticed as he stepped out into the night air was how completely calm and quiet it was. Not a single leaf was moving.

Terry walked to the corner of his house and as soon as he turned that corner the weight of the world lifted off his shoulders. There, above the tree in his yard were three angels, all in white, whose wings were moving ever so slightly to keep them afloat. The angels to the left and right were both faceless. The angel in the middle was Troy, looking down and smiling at him just as he had looked the last time they were together.

At that moment I had total confirmation that my prayers had been answered. God had taken care of my son. We believe Troy continues to give me and others strength and gifts on a regular basis. We are truly blessed with our very own special guardian angel.

I've had many questions since that day but never once have I questioned the validity of this story. I know it happened. I could not only tell by the glow on Terry's face as he was telling me but by the way my heart felt since the accident. I just knew Troy was still with me.

Terry is so blessed to have received this visit. It had to happen this way. Had I received it I don't think I would've been believed. I'm so thankful that God allowed Terry to confirm His answer to my prayer.

Maybe Troy was accompanied by angels all along, sent down to earth that night when I was only nineteen years old and needing someone special in my life. Perhaps he was sent to confirm a famous bible story for the world to hear again so we will know He is here.

It is the Resurrection question: The book of Mark: Chapter 12; Verses 18 thru 27

Some Sadducees, who say there is no resurrection,
came to Jesus and put this question to him,
saying, "Teacher, Moses wrote for us, 'If
someone's brother dies, leaving a wife but no
child, his brother must take the wife and raise
up descendants for his brother.' Now there were
seven brothers. The first married a woman and
died, leaving no descendants. So the second
married her and died, leaving no descendants
and the third likewise. And the seven left no
descendants. Finally, the woman also died. At the
resurrection (when they arise) whose wife will
she be? For all seven had been married to her."
Jesus said to them, "Are you not misled because
you do not know the scriptures or the power of
God? When they rise from the dead, they neither
marry nor are given in marriage, but they are like
the angels in heaven.

Epilogue

As I was thinking about writing this book one day I logged onto my computer and proceeded to type a couple of paragraphs. That's as far as I got. I just wasn't ready. So I closed out the program. This is what popped up on my computer screen in the top left corner. It says, "Troy's Miracles" with TROY underneath. It looked as if someone would be helping me write this book. I took a picture.

Mom, Kimble and I took a trip down to South Carolina in April to see my sister Janice and her husband Audie. They took us on several tours while we were there; Charleston, South Carolina and Savannah, Georgia being wonderful all day trips. I enjoyed seeing the large historical homes on the coast of Charleston but I immediately fell in love with the Savannah River walk.

Meandering along the cobblestone roadway that runs along the Savannah River I felt like I was home. Perhaps it reminded me of the countless days I'd sat and watched the Ohio River rippling in the breeze and the comfort it brought me. I could've spent the whole day just running in and out of the River Street Sweets shop sampling their free bites of the world famous pralines. If you're a sweet fanatic like I am, one bite of a praline and you will think you've died and gone to heaven!

Audie and Janice were anxious to show us some more of the city so I made sure I had a sack of pralines in tow before they drug me away. After a quick tour around the historic district we were ready to head to the Market Place. Since they had visited only once before, Audie thought we were pretty close when he spotted a rare parking spot. Oh so proud of himself, he swung into an alley and backed right into the spot like a pro.

As we hopped out of the vehicle I noticed a gentleman adjacent to us, standing next to a building that seemed to be less than fascinated with our quick entry. Woops. Janice and I sauntered up to the window he was standing next to where I observed a couple of books on display.

When Elvis Meets the Dalai Lama looked nice but it was the cover of *Behind the Moss Curtain* that drew my attention. Looked like a spirit was visiting from the past; I thought of Harvey.

Turned out the man standing next to me was the writer, Murray Silver Jr., the famous author of *Great Balls of Fire: the Uncensored Story of Jerry Lee Lewis,* which was made into a movie. I told him about Harvey.

While Murray was autographing my purchase mom was commenting that I should move to Savannah since I liked it so much. I informed her I was perfectly happy where I was and Murray added that the women he knew who had moved down there had no trouble finding jobs. I said, "You never know, there are no coincidences."

I thanked him for the autograph and was halfway out the door when I heard, "What do you want to do?" I turned around, again Murray said, "What do you want to do?" The third time he asked me I said, "Write a book!"

Well, I don't know who said that? First of all it had nothing to do with the subject he was asking about and second of all it's totally out of character for me to divulge a secret like that to anyone, much less a man I'd just met!

So then Murray tells me he'll help me publish it. Huh? Well, okay, back in the store I go. Of course mom and Janice heard all this so now my secret desire was a secret no more and I knew at that very moment I was going to write this book.

Murray gave me a contact phone number and the rest of the day I replayed the events over and over in my head. We finally found the Market Place and a parking spot. I hadn't walked but a few feet when I spotted a heads up penny so naturally I picked it up. It was dated 1973. It didn't surprise me. Was it a sign Troy had set the meeting up with Murray? Maybe it was.

As it turns out Murray was born on October 3, the day mom said I was scheduled to drop into the world but thanks to a doctor who sent her back home I showed up two days late. Heck, God probably planned all this before Murray and I were born!

Really, what are the chances? We pop into a parking spot way away from where we're supposed to be; find a guy autographing his books who offers to help publish mine and we were practically born on the same day?

I believe God wants us to know He is still here for us, closer than we realize. If we just talk to Him, trust Him completely, and wait for things to happen in His time instead of ours He will take care of us. There are no coincidences.

Top left: Baby Troy
Above: Troy and Terry
Left: Troy Boy Scout

Top: First Communion
To Right: Over the Top
Right: Track

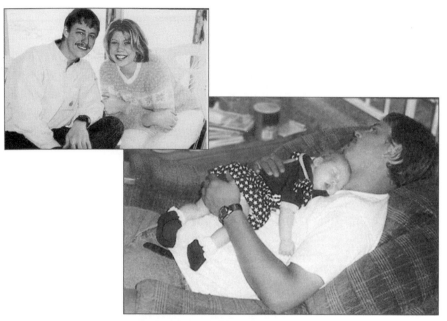

Top left: Troy and Shayna

Top Right: Troy and Jaidan

Left: Terra, Me, Troy

About Terry Lee Rambo

Terry Lee Rambo was the first of five children born in a small western Kentucky town to a very special mom and an abusive father. Fifty-six years later-- after many moves, three husbands and two children-- she found herself alone in Indiana. Her daughter had moved far away, her husband of thirty years had divorced her, and her first born died in an automobile accident at age 28.

But was she really alone? Within these pages is what she believes is the irrefutable proof that her prayers were answered and that her son remains on Earth as her angel. The miracles and gifts that Terry continues to receive give her a tremendous feeling of peace and the reassurance that our children are with us forever!

This is her first book.

She is available for speeches and book signings. Please contact her at **TerryLee53@gmail.com**